How to use your Snap Revision

This 'Romeo and Juliet' Snap Workbook will help yo
mark in your AQA English Literature exam. Question
grouped into plot; setting and context; characters; themes; and exam
practice, and are designed to help you fully prepare for the exam.

Revise 1, 2 and 3
Short tasks progressing
in level as you work
through the topic.

Extend
Longer, essay-style
questions to be
completed on separate
pieces of paper.

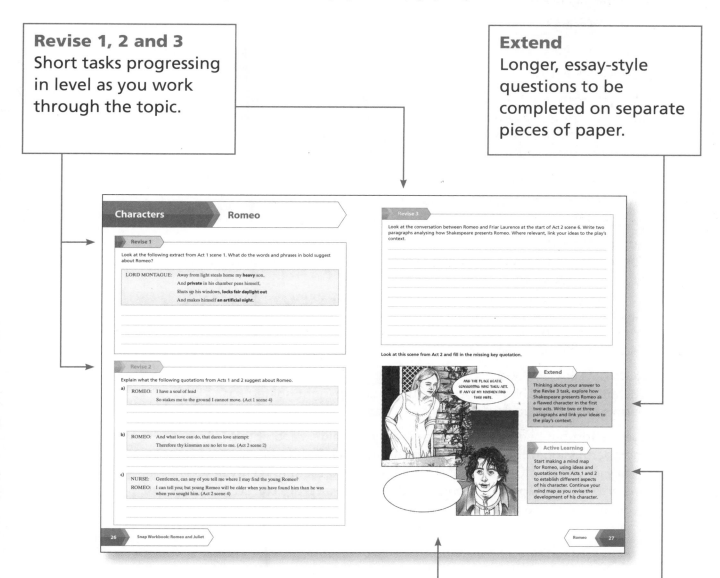

Answers
Provided at the back
of the book.

Comic strips
Show key scenes from
the text and include
blank speech bubbles
for you to fill in the
missing key quotations
from memory.

Active learning
Interactive tasks such
as creating posters,
storyboards and
mind maps.

AUTHOR: IAN KIRBY

Published by Collins
An imprint of HarperCollins*Publishers*
1 London Bridge Street
London SE1 9GF

© HarperCollins*Publishers* Limited 2021

ISBN 9780008437398

First published 2021

10 9 8 7 6 5 4 3 2 1

British Library Cataloguing in Publication Data.

A CIP record of this book is available from the British Library.

Commissioning: Sundus Pasha and Richard Toms
Author: Ian Kirby
Copyeditor and project management: Fiona Watson and Lauren Murray
Typesetting: Jouve India Private Limited
Cover designers: Kneath Associates and Sarah Duxbury
Illustrations: Rose and Thorn Creative Services Ltd
Production: Karen Nulty
Printed in the UK by Martins the Printer Ltd

ACKNOWLEDGEMENTS
The author and publisher are grateful to the copyright holders for permission to use quoted materials and images.

Every effort has been made to trace copyright holders and obtain their permission for the use of copyright material. The author and publisher will gladly receive information enabling them to rectify any error or omission in subsequent editions. All facts are correct at time of going to press.

MIX
Paper from
responsible sources

FSC
www.fsc.org   **FSC™ C007454**

This book is produced from independently certified FSC™ paper to ensure responsible forest management.

For more information visit:
www.harpercollins.co.uk/green

Contents

Revise 1

Number the following statements about the plot to show the correct order:

☐ Lord and Lady Montague are worried about their son, Romeo; he reveals to his friend, Benvolio, that he is suffering from unrequited love for a girl called Rosaline.

☐ A fight between the Capulets and the Montagues is stopped by Prince Escalus.

☐ Lord Capulet and Paris discuss Paris's wish to marry Juliet; Capulet feels his daughter is too young to get married.

☐ A sonnet summarises the events of the play, creating a sense of fate and tragedy.

Revise 2

Select and explain some quotations from Act 1 scene 1 that show Romeo's feelings.

_____

_____

_____

_____

_____

_____

_____

_____

_____

_____

_____

_____

Look at Act 1 scene 2, where Capulet and Paris are talking. Write two paragraphs analysing how Shakespeare presents Lord Capulet's thoughts and feelings for his daughter, Juliet. Where relevant, link your ideas to the play's context.

....

....

....

....

....

....

....

....

....

....

> Extend

Explore how Shakespeare presents different conflicts at the start of the play. Consider physical conflict as well as conflicts of emotions and attitudes. Write two or three paragraphs and link your ideas to the play's context.

> Active Learning

Start making a record of the play's key moments and quotations. This could be a learning poster, a mobile, different cue cards, or a changing screensaver on your phone or tablet. Keep developing it as you revise each act.

Look at this scene from Act 1 and fill in the missing key quotation.

I DO BUT KEEP THE PEACE: PUT UP THY SWORD, OR MANAGE IT TO PART THESE MEN WITH ME.

WHAT, DRAWN, AND TALK OF PEACE?

Revise 1

Number the following statements about the plot to show the correct order:

☐ Tybalt is angry that Romeo is at the feast; he wants to fight him but is stopped by Lord Capulet.

☐ As soon as he sees Juliet at the Capulets' feast, Romeo falls in love with her.

☐ Romeo and Juliet talk and kiss. Once they have parted, they realise that each is from their rival family.

☐ Lady Capulet encourages Juliet to think about getting married.

Revise 2

Explain what the following quotations from Act 1 scene 5 suggest about Romeo's thoughts and feelings.

a)

> ROMEO: O, she doth teach the torches to burn bright!

....

....

....

....

....

b)

> ROMEO: Did my heart love till now? Forswear it, sight! / For I ne'er saw true beauty till this night.

....

....

....

....

c)

> ROMEO: Is she a Capulet? / O dear account! My life is my foe's debt.

....

....

....

....

Look at Act 1 scene 3. Write two paragraphs analysing how Shakespeare shows Lady Capulet trying to convince Juliet to think about marriage. Where relevant, link your ideas to the play's context.

Extend

Look at the sonnet that Romeo and Juliet share in Act 1 scene 5 (starting with 'If I profane …' and ending with their kiss). Write two or three paragraphs exploring how Shakespeare presents the love between Romeo and Juliet. Link your ideas to the play's context.

Active Learning

Create a learning poster for Act 1, depicting the different thoughts and feelings shown by Romeo.

Look at this scene from Act 1 and fill in the missing key quotation.

Revise 1

Number the following statements about the plot to show the correct order:

☐ Juliet talks of her wish that Romeo wasn't a Montague.

☐ Romeo and Juliet say they love each other; she suggests they marry the next day.

☐ Romeo returns to the Capulet house and watches Juliet on her balcony.

☐ Friar Laurence agrees to join the two lovers in marriage.

Revise 2

Looking at Act 2 scene 3, explain Friar Laurence's thoughts and feelings about Romeo's wish to marry Juliet. Use brief quotations to support your ideas.

Look at Act 2 scene 2. Write one paragraph analysing how Shakespeare conveys Romeo's love for Juliet, and one paragraph analysing how he conveys Juliet's love for Romeo. Where relevant, link your ideas to the play's context.

Look at this scene from Act 2 and fill in the missing key quotation.

WHAT'S IN A NAME?

Extend

Thinking about your response to the Revise 3 task, explore how Shakespeare uses references to fate and death in Romeo and Juliet's dialogue in Act 2 scene 2. Link your ideas to the play's context.

Active Learning

Pick out the different metaphors that Shakespeare uses at the start of Act 2 scene 2 to convey Romeo's thoughts and feelings as he watches Juliet. Present the words and their meaning in picture form.

Revise 1

Number the following statements about the plot to show the correct order:

☐ Romeo and Juliet meet with Friar Laurence to be married.

☐ Juliet anxiously awaits a message from Romeo which the Nurse eventually gives her.

☐ Romeo asks the Nurse to pass on a message to Juliet, confirming their marriage later that day.

☐ Romeo jokes with his friends, Mercutio and Benvolio, but doesn't tell them about Juliet.

Revise 2

In Act 2 scene 4, Mercutio describes Romeo's unrequited love for Rosaline as well as the news that Tybalt has sent a challenge to Romeo. Commenting on specific words and phrases, explain how Romeo is presented in the following quotation:

> Alas, poor Romeo, he is already dead! stabbed with a white wench's black eye; shot through the ear with a love song; the very pin of his heart cleft with the blind bow-boy's butt-shaft. And is he a man to encounter Tybalt?

Looking at Act 2 scene 5, write two paragraphs analysing how Shakespeare presents the relationship between the Nurse and Juliet. Where relevant, link your ideas to the play's context.

_____

_____

_____

_____

_____

_____

_____

_____

Look at this scene from Act 2 and fill in the missing key quotation.

DO THOU BUT CLOSE OUR HANDS WITH HOLY WORDS,

Extend

Starting with Act 2 scene 6, write two or three paragraphs exploring how Shakespeare presents the idea that Romeo and Juliet are rushing their relationship. Link your ideas to the play's context.

Active Learning

Looking at Act 2 scene 4, create a learning poster that depicts how Mercutio talks about Tybalt and the Nurse. Use images and quotations. Highlight any similar language being used.

Revise 1

Number the following statements about the plot to show the correct order:

☐ A group of Montagues and Capulets meet; Tybalt and Mercutio begin to argue.

☐ Prince Escalus pronounces Romeo's banishment from Verona.

☐ Romeo tries to stop the fight, resulting in Mercutio being stabbed by Tybalt. In revenge, Romeo kills Tybalt.

☐ Romeo arrives but refuses to fight Tybalt so Mercutio fights him instead.

Revise 2

Looking at the following quotations from Act 3 scene 1, explain Romeo's different reactions to Tybalt.

a)

ROMEO:	I do protest, I never injured thee,
	But love thee better than thou canst devise …

b)

ROMEO:	Away to heaven, respective lenity,
	And fire-ey'd fury be my conduct now!

c)

ROMEO:	Either thou, or I, or both, must go with him.

Look at Juliet's speech in Act 3 scene 2, beginning 'O serpent heart …'

Write two paragraphs analysing how Shakespeare presents Juliet's thoughts and feelings when she discovers that Romeo has killed Tybalt. Where relevant, link your ideas to the play's context.

....

....

....

....

....

....

....

....

....

....

Look at this scene from Act 3 and fill in the missing key quotation.

I AM HURT.

Revise 1

Number the following statements about the plot to show the correct order:

☐ Juliet angers her parents by refusing to marry Paris; the Nurse advises her to forget Romeo.

☐ Lord Capulet decides that Juliet should marry Paris in three days' time.

☐ Friar Laurence brings news to Romeo that he has been banished from Verona.

☐ Romeo and Juliet spend their wedding night together and reluctantly part in the morning.

Revise 2

Using the following quotations from Act 3 scene 3, explain Romeo's response to the news of his banishment.

a)

> ROMEO: … calling death 'banishment',
>
> Thou cut'st my head off with a golden axe,
>
> And smilest upon the stroke that murders me.

....

....

....

b)

> ROMEO: 'Tis torture, and not mercy: heaven is here,
>
> Where Juliet lives …

....

....

....

c)

> ROMEO: It helps not, it prevails not: talk no more.

....

....

....

Looking at Act 3 scene 5, write two paragraphs analysing how Shakespeare shows Lord Capulet's reaction to Juliet's refusal to marry Paris. Where relevant, link your ideas to the play's context.

....

....

....

....

....

....

....

....

....

....

....

....

....

Look at this scene from Act 3 and fill in the missing key quotation.

WOULD NONE BUT I MIGHT VENGE MY COUSIN'S DEATH.

Extend

Thinking about your response to the Revise 3 task, write two or three paragraphs exploring how Lady Capulet's response to her daughter's refusal is presented similarly or differently to her husband's response. Link your ideas to the play's context.

Active Learning

Write a diary, from the perspective of Lady Capulet, based on Act 3 scene 5. Consider her thoughts about Juliet, Paris, Tybalt, Romeo and Lord Capulet.

Revise 1

Number the following statements about the plot to show the correct order:

☐ Juliet apologises to her father for her disobedience.

☐ Lord Capulet brings forward the marriage by a day and Juliet takes the Friar's potion.

☐ Friar Laurence outlines his plan for Juliet to fake her death so Romeo can collect her and take her back to Mantua.

☐ Juliet is found, apparently dead, by the Nurse; her parents are distraught.

Revise 2

Looking at Act 4 scene 3, select three quotations that show Juliet's thoughts or feelings before she takes the potion. Explain each of your choices.

_____

_____

_____

_____

_____

_____

_____

_____

_____

_____

_____

_____

_____

Looking at Act 4 scene 5, write a paragraph analysing how Shakespeare presents Lady Capulet's response to Juliet's apparent death, and a paragraph about Lord Capulet's response. Where relevant, link your ideas to the play's context.

Look at this scene from Act 4 and fill in the missing key quotation.

O LAMENTABLE DAY!

O WOEFUL TIME!

Thinking about your response to the Revise 3 task, compare how Lord Capulet, Lady Capulet or the Nurse respond to Juliet in Act 4 scene 5 and in Act 3 scene 5.

Create a poster depicting the reasons why Juliet fakes her death and the things that almost stop her. Use quotations and images to support your ideas.

Plot

Act 5

Revise 1

Number the following statements about the plot to show the correct order:

☐ Romeo and Paris fight outside Juliet's tomb and Paris is killed.

☐ Romeo lays down by Juliet and drinks the poison; waking, Juliet finds Romeo dead and stabs herself.

☐ Romeo is brought news of Juliet's death; knowing nothing of Friar Laurence's plan, he buys poison and makes his way to Juliet's tomb.

☐ At the sight of their dead children, Lord Capulet and Lord Montague are reconciled.

Revise 2

Looking at Romeo's soliloquy from the start of Act 5, underline the words and phrases that make Romeo sound happy and hopeful that he'll be reunited with Juliet. Explain your choices and also consider how the soliloquy foreshadows Romeo's death.

ROMEO: If I may trust the flattering truth of sleep,

My dreams presage some joyful news at hand.

My bosom's lord sits lightly in his throne;

And all this day an unaccustom'd spirit

Lifts me above the ground with cheerful thoughts.

I dreamt my lady came and found me dead –

Strange dream, that gives a dead man leave to think! –

And breath'd such life with kisses in my lips,

That I reviv'd and was an emperor.

Ah me! how sweet is love itself possess'd,

When but love's shadows are so rich in joy!

_____

_____

_____

_____

Looking at Act 5 scene 3, write two paragraphs analysing how Shakespeare presents Romeo's combination of love and grief when he enters the tomb and sees Juliet. Where relevant, link your ideas to the play's context.

....

....

....

....

....

....

....

....

Look at this scene from Act 5 and fill in the missing key quotation.

Extend

Continuing with Act 5 scene 3, write two or three paragraphs exploring how the tragedy of Romeo's and Juliet's deaths are presented through the language of their parents and Prince Escalus. Link your ideas to the play's context.

Active Learning

Create a comic strip or storyboard showing the different events of Act 5 and suggesting how much time passes between each event. Use quotations to support your images.

Revise 1

Indicate whether the following statements about the play's Italian setting, around the 14th century, are true or false.

a) The play is set in Rome. ....

b) Arranged marriages were unusual. ....

c) There was inequality between the genders. ....

d) The Catholic faith was very important. ....

Revise 2

Explain the following aspects of Italian society around the 14th century and their significance to the play.

a) Religion

....

....

....

....

b) Patriarchy

....

....

....

....

c) Status

....

....

....

....

Re-read Act 3 scene 4. Write two paragraphs analysing how Shakespeare uses attitudes to marriage to show the change in Lord Capulet.

_____
_____
_____
_____
_____
_____
_____
_____
_____
_____
_____
_____
_____
_____
_____
_____
_____
_____

Extend

Re-read Act 3 scene 5, from Lady Capulet's entrance ('Ho, daughter! Are you up?'). Write two or three paragraphs exploring how Shakespeare uses different contextual attitudes to create conflict within the Capulet family.

Active Learning

Create a visual representation of the different social groups that Shakespeare includes in the play. It might help to start by thinking about which group you would allocate the following characters to: Lord Capulet, the Nurse and Friar Laurence.

Revise 1

Indicate whether the following statements about Elizabeth I and Renaissance England, when Shakespeare was writing the play, are true or false.

a) Elizabeth I ruled during a time of peace and prosperity in England. _____

b) At the time, the English considered Italy to be a fashionable country. _____

c) There were major outbreaks of plague in the second half of the 16th century. _____

d) On stage in Renaissance England, female characters were played by men. _____

Revise 2

Explain how the conflicts in the play might reflect the conflict that Shakespeare would have been aware of in Renaissance England. Use quotations to support your ideas.

_____

_____

_____

_____

_____

_____

_____

_____

_____

_____

_____

_____

Looking at Act 1 scene 3, write two paragraphs analysing how the Nurse is used as a comic character to appeal to the Elizabethan audience.

Extend

Thinking about your response to the Revise 3 task, write two or three paragraphs exploring how Mercutio is used to create rude humour to appeal to the less refined members of the Elizabethan audience.

Active Learning

Develop your understanding of the play's context by researching the following topics:

a) The Wars of the Roses

b) The Rose Theatre

c) Theatre audiences in Elizabethan England

d) Plague in Elizabethan England.

Turn your findings into a report, a PowerPoint presentation or a poster.

Revise 1

Define what is meant by a play being a tragedy.

Revise 2

Using the following extracts as a starting point, explain the effects of some of Shakespeare's stagecraft techniques.

a) Soliloquies

> JULIET: My dismal scene I needs must act alone.
>
> Come, vial.
>
> What if this mixture do not work at all? (Act 4 scene 3)

b) Disguise

> ROMEO: What lady is that, which doth enrich the hand
>
> Of yonder knight?
>
> SERVANT: I know not, sir.
>
> ROMEO: O, she doth teach the torches to burn bright! (Act 1 scene 5)

c) Violence

> PARIS: I do defy thy conjurations,
>
> And apprehend thee for a felon here.
>
> ROMEO: Wilt thou provoke me? Then have at thee, boy! *[They fight]* (Act 5 scene 3)

Re-read the Prologue. Write two paragraphs analysing how Shakespeare uses language to establish the play as a tragedy.

_____

_____

_____

_____

_____

_____

_____

_____

_____

_____

_____

_____

_____

_____

_____

_____

Extend

Write two or three paragraphs exploring a point in the play where Shakespeare uses changes in mood to highlight the play's tragedy. For example, you might explore the first half of Act 3 scene 1, the contrast between the end of Act 3 scene 1 and the start of Act 3 scene 2, or the contrast between Act 4 scene 4 and Act 4 scene 5.

Active Learning

Using the internet, research one specific element of stagecraft in different productions of _Romeo and Juliet_. For example, you could explore the use of soliloquy, concealment and movement in Act 2 scene 2, or the staging of Romeo's and Juliet's deaths in Act 5 scene 3.

Revise 1

Look at the following extract from Act 1 scene 1. What do the words and phrases in bold suggest about Romeo?

> LORD MONTAGUE: Away from light steals home my **heavy** son,
>
> And **private** in his chamber pens himself,
>
> Shuts up his windows, **locks fair daylight out**
>
> And makes himself **an artificial night**.

....

....

....

....

Revise 2

Explain what the following quotations from Acts 1 and 2 suggest about Romeo.

a)
> ROMEO: I have a soul of lead
>
> So stakes me to the ground I cannot move. (Act 1 scene 4)

....

....

b)
> ROMEO: And what love can do, that dares love attempt:
>
> Therefore thy kinsman are no let to me. (Act 2 scene 2)

....

....

c)
> NURSE: Gentlemen, can any of you tell me where I may find the young Romeo?
>
> ROMEO: I can tell you; but young Romeo will be older when you have found him than he was when you sought him. (Act 2 scene 4)

....

....

Look at the conversation between Romeo and Friar Laurence at the start of Act 2 scene 6. Write two paragraphs analysing how Shakespeare presents Romeo. Where relevant, link your ideas to the play's context.

....

....

....

....

....

....

....

....

....

Look at this scene from Act 2 and fill in the missing key quotation.

AND THE PLACE DEATH, CONSIDERING WHO THOU ART, IF ANY OF MY KINSMEN FIND THEE HERE.

Thinking about your answer to the Revise 3 task, explore how Shakespeare presents Romeo as a flawed character in the first two acts. Write two or three paragraphs and link your ideas to the play's context.

Start making a mind map for Romeo, using ideas and quotations from Acts 1 and 2 to establish different aspects of his character. Continue your mind map as you revise the development of his character.

Revise 1

Select two quotations from Act 3 that show Romeo's response to being banished.

Revise 2

Explain how the following quotations show different sides of Romeo's character.

a)

ROMEO: [to Tybalt]   And so, good Capulet, which name I tender

As dearly as mine own, be satisfied. (Act 3 scene 1)

b)

ROMEO: O sweet Juliet,

Thy beauty hath made me effeminate

And in my temper soften'd valour's steel! (Act 3 scene 1)

c)

ROMEO: [to Juliet]   More light and light: more dark and dark our woes. (Act 3 scene 5)

Looking at Romeo's soliloquy in Act 5 scene 3 before he kills himself, write two paragraphs analysing how Shakespeare presents Romeo's love for Juliet. Where relevant, link your ideas to the play's context.

....

....

....

....

....

....

....

....

....

Look at this scene from Act 3 and fill in the missing key quotation.

O DEADLY SIN! O RUDE UNTHANKFULNESS!

Extend

Thinking about your response to the Revise 3 task, write two or three paragraphs exploring how Shakespeare presents Romeo as increasingly reckless and desperate in Act 3 scene 3 and Act 5 scenes 1 and 3. Link your ideas to the play's context.

Active Learning

Create a visual flow diagram illustrating the key scenes in the play that lead to Romeo's death.

Revise 1

In Act 1 scene 3, Juliet describes marriage as 'an honour that I dream not of'. What does this tell us about Juliet and the effect that Romeo will have on her?

....

....

....

....

Revise 2

Explain what the following quotations suggest about Juliet and her relationships with others.

a)

> JULIET: [to her mother]   Madam, I am here.
>
>   What is your will? (Act 1 scene 3)

....

....

b)

> JULIET: [to the Nurse, about Romeo] Go ask his name. If he be married,
>
>   My grave is like to be my wedding bed. (Act 1 scene 5)

....

....

c)

> JULIET: [thinking about Romeo]   be but sworn my love,
>
>   And I'll no longer be a Capulet. (Act 2 scene 2)

....

....

Look at Juliet's speech in Act 2 scene 2, from 'Well, do not swear' to 'Yet I should kill thee with much cherishing'. Write two paragraphs analysing how Shakespeare presents different sides of Juliet's character. Where relevant, link your ideas to the play's context.

....

....

....

....

....

....

....

....

Look at this scene from Act 2 and fill in the missing key quotation.

OR, IF THOU WILT NOT, BE BUT SWORN MY LOVE, AND I'LL NO LONGER BE A CAPULET.

Extend

Thinking about your answer to the Revise 3 task, explore where else Shakespeare presents contradictory aspects of Juliet's character in the first two acts. Link your ideas to the play's context.

Active Learning

Start making a mind map for Juliet, using ideas from Acts 1 and 2 to establish different aspects of her character. Continue your mind map as you revise the development of her character.

Revise 1

Explain how these lines from Act 3 scene 2 show Juliet's love for Romeo.

> JULIET: Come, gentle night, come, loving black-brow'd night,
>
> Give me my Romeo.

_____

_____

_____

Revise 2

Explain what the following quotations suggest about Juliet's feelings for Romeo at different points in Act 3.

a)

> JULIET: O break, my heart! Poor bankrupt, break at once!
>
> To prison, eyes, ne'er look on liberty! (Act 3 scene 2)

_____

_____

_____

b)

> JULIET: [to Romeo]   Art thou gone so? Love, lord, ay husband, friend!
>
> I must hear from thee every day in the hour,
>
> For in a minute there are many days. (Act 3 scene 5)

_____

_____

_____

c)

> JULIET: [to Lady Capulet]   Indeed, I never shall be satisfied
>
> With Romeo, till I behold him – dead –
>
> Is my poor heart so for a kinsman vex'd. (Act 3 scene 5)

_____

_____

_____

Write two paragraphs analysing how Shakespeare presents Juliet's thoughts and feelings when talking to Friar Laurence in Act 4 scene 1. Where relevant, link your ideas to the play's context.

....

....

....

....

....

....

....

....

....

....

Look at this scene from Act 5 and fill in the missing key quotation.

THERE RUST, AND LET ME DIE.

Extend

Thinking about your response to the Revise 3 task, write two or three paragraphs exploring how Juliet is presented as alone and desperate in Act 3 scene 5 and Act 4 scene 3. Link your ideas to the play's context.

Active Learning

Create a learning poster illustrating how far different characters affect Juliet's decisions and behaviour. Consider the influence of Romeo, Lord and Lady Capulet, the Nurse and Friar Laurence. Use quotations to support your ideas.

Revise 1

Explain what the following quotation from Act 1 scene 4 suggests about Mercutio and his relationship with Romeo.

ROMEO:	Under love's heavy burden do I sink.
MERCUTIO:	And, to sink in it, should you burden love –
	Too great oppression for a tender thing.

....

....

....

....

Revise 2

Explain how Shakespeare uses Mercutio to create humour in the following quotations.

a)

MERCUTIO:	Now will he sit under a medlar tree,
	And wish his mistress were that kind of fruit …
	O Romeo, that she were, O that she were
	An open-arse and thou a poperin pear! (Act 2 scene 1)

....

....

....

b)

MERCUTIO: [singing]	But a hare that is hoar
	Is too much for a score
	When it hoars ere it be spent. (Act 2 scene 4)

....

....

....

Write two paragraphs analysing how Shakespeare presents Mercutio after he has been stabbed in Act 3 scene 1. Where relevant, link your ideas to the play's context.

....

....

....

....

....

....

....

....

....

....

Look at this scene from Act 2 and fill in the missing key quotation.

FAREWELL, ANCIENT LADY, FAREWELL, LADY, LADY, LADY.

A GENTLEMAN, NURSE, THAT LOVES TO HEAR HIMSELF TALK, AND WILL SPEAK MORE IN A MINUTE THAN HE WILL STAND TO IN A MONTH.

Extend

Thinking about your response to the Revise 3 task, explore how Shakespeare uses language and the play's structure to make Mercutio a tragic character. Write two or three paragraphs and link your ideas to the play's context.

Active Learning

Make a mind map for Mercutio, showing different aspects of his character.

Revise 1

How does Shakespeare present Tybalt in the following quotation from Act 1 scene 1?

> TYBALT: What, art thou drawn among these heartless hinds?
>
> Turn thee, Benvolio, look upon thy death.

Revise 2

Explain how Tybalt is presented during his interaction with Lord Capulet in Act 1 scene 5. Support your ideas with quotations.

Looking at Act 3 scene 1, write two paragraphs analysing how Shakespeare presents different sides of Tybalt's character. Where relevant, link your ideas to the play's context.

_____

_____

_____

_____

_____

_____

_____

_____

_____

_____

Look at this scene from Act 3 and fill in the missing key quotation.

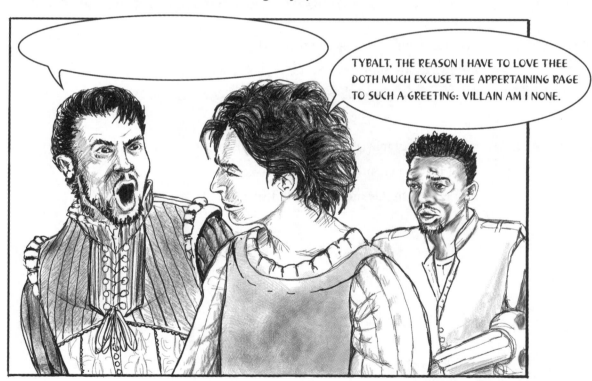

TYBALT, THE REASON I HAVE TO LOVE THEE DOTH MUCH EXCUSE THE APPERTAINING RAGE TO SUCH A GREETING: VILLAIN AM I NONE.

Extend

Thinking about your answer to the Revise 3 task, explore how Shakespeare uses other characters in the play to present the different sides of Tybalt's character. Write two or three paragraphs and link your ideas to the play's context.

Active Learning

Make a mind map for Tybalt, using ideas and quotations from Acts 1 to 3 to show different aspects of his character.

Revise 1

What can you work out about Lord and Lady Capulet from their opening exchange?

> LORD CAPULET: What noise is this? Give me my long sword, ho!
>
> LADY CAPULET: A crutch, a crutch! Why call you for a sword?

Revise 2

Explain how the two quotations below show the differences between Lord and Lady Capulet.

> LORD CAPULET: My child is yet a stranger in the world …
>
> Let two more summers whither in their pride
>
> Ere we make think her ripe to be a bride. (Act 1 scene 2)
>
> LADY CAPULET: Well, think of marriage now. Younger than you,
>
> Here in Verona, ladies of esteem,
>
> Are made already mothers. (Act 1 scene 3)

Analyse how Shakespeare presents Lady Capulet as vengeful. Write one paragraph using Act 3 scene 1 and another using Act 3 scene 5. Where relevant, link your ideas to the play's context.

....

....

....

....

....

....

....

....

Look at this scene from Act 3 and fill in the missing key quotation.

HOW NOW, WIFE! HAVE YOU DELIVER'D TO HER OUR DECREE?

AY SIR, BUT SHE WILL NONE, SHE GIVES YOU THANKS.

Write two or three paragraphs exploring how Shakespeare presents Lord Capulet as the head of the house. Consider where he seems more powerful or important than other members of his family. Link your ideas to the play's context.

Make mind maps for Lord and Lady Capulet, using ideas and quotations to show different aspects of their characters.

Revise 1

Explain how the following quotation from Act 5 scene 3 shows Paris's love for Juliet.

> PARIS: Sweet flower, with flowers thy bridal bed I strew.
>
> O woe! thy canopy is dust and stones
>
> Which with sweet water nightly I will dew,
>
> Or, wanting that, with tears distill'd by moans.

Revise 2

Looking at Act 1 scene 3, find and explain quotations that show the following things about the Nurse:

a) her opinion of Paris

b) her affection for Juliet

c) her lower-class status.

Look at the Nurse's interaction with Romeo at the end of Act 2 scene 4 (from 'I pray you, sir').
Write one paragraph analysing how Shakespeare presents the Nurse as a comic figure and another
analysing how she is given a serious side. Where relevant, link your ideas to the play's context.

Look at this scene from Act 3 and fill in the missing key quotation.

ROMEO'S A DISHCLOUT TO HIM:
AN EAGLE, MADAM,
HATH NOT SO GREEN, SO QUICK,
SO FAIR AN EYE
AS PARIS HATH.

Extend

Thinking about your response to
the Revise 3 task, explore how
the Nurse is presented as both
comic and serious elsewhere in
the play. You might refer to Act 1
scene 3, Act 2 scene 5 and Act 4
scene 5.

Active Learning

Make mind maps for Paris and
the Nurse, using ideas and
quotations to show different
aspects of their characters.

Characters

Revise 1

What do the following lines from Act 1 scene 1 suggest about Benvolio and his relationship with Romeo?

ROMEO:	Dost thou not laugh?
BENVOLIO:	No, coz, I rather weep.
ROMEO:	Good heart, at what?
BENVOLIO:	At thy good heart's oppression.

....

....

....

....

Revise 2

Look at Act 3 scene 1. Select and explain quotations that show how the play presents the following conflicting impressions of Benvolio:

a) Peaceful yet quarrelsome

....

....

....

....

....

b) Honourable yet untrustworthy

....

....

....

....

....

Look at Friar Laurence's speech at the end of Act 5 (beginning 'I will be brief'). Write a paragraph analysing how the Friar is presented as defending his actions and a paragraph on how he admits his guilt. Where relevant, link your ideas to the play's context.

Look at this scene from Act 2 and fill in the missing key quotation.

Considering your response to the Revise 3 task, explore how far Shakespeare presents Friar Laurence as displaying poor judgement. Write two or three paragraphs and relate your ideas to the play's context. You might refer to Act 2 scenes 3 and 6, Act 3 scene 3, Act 4 scene 1 and Act 5 scene 3.

Make mind maps for Benvolio and Friar Laurence, using ideas and quotations to show different aspects of their characters.

Themes   Love

Revise 1

Which characters are linked to love in the play? What kind of obstacles does their love come up against?

_____

_____

_____

_____

_____

_____

Revise 2

Looking at Act 2 scene 2, select and explain three quotations that suggest true love is **a)** beautiful, **b)** powerful and **c)** impulsive.

_____

_____

_____

_____

_____

_____

_____

_____

_____

_____

_____

Looking at Act 1 scene 5, write two paragraphs analysing how Shakespeare uses religious imagery to present true love. Where relevant, link your ideas to the play's context.

_____

_____

_____

_____

_____

_____

_____

_____

_____

_____

Look at this scene from Act 2 and fill in the missing key quotation.

SLEEP DWELL UPON THINE EYES, PEACE IN THY BREAST!

Write two or three paragraphs exploring how Shakespeare presents love as causing pain. Link your ideas to the play's context.

Create a learning poster on the theme of love, including clear references to characters, key scenes and useful quotations.

Revise 1

Which characters are linked to conflict and what are the different consequences of these conflicts?

....

....

....

....

Revise 2

Explain how the following quotations show comic, tragic and family conflict.

a)

> GREGORY: Do you quarrel, sir?
>
> ABRAHAM: Quarrel, sir? No, sir.
>
> SAMPSON: But if you do, sir, I am for you. (Act 1 scene 1)

....

....

....

b)

> MERCUTIO: A plague o' both your houses!
>
> They have made worms' meat of me. (Act 3 scene 1)

....

....

....

c)

> LORD CAPULET: Hang thee young baggage! disobedient wretch! (Act 3 scene 5)

....

....

....

....

Analyse how Shakespeare presents conflict as being linked to honour in Act 3 scene 1. Write two paragraphs and, where relevant, link your ideas to the play's context.

....

....

....

....

....

....

....

....

Look at this scene from Act 5 and fill in the missing key quotation.

Extend

Thinking about your response to the Revise 3 task, explore how conflict is linked to honour elsewhere in the play. Write two or three paragraphs and link your ideas to the play's context. You could consider Act 1 scenes 1 and 5, Act 3 scene 5 and Act 5 scene 3.

Active Learning

Create a learning poster on the theme of conflict, including clear references to characters, key scenes and useful quotations.

Revise 1

Match the quotations below to the different techniques used by Shakespeare to convey Romeo's inner turmoil.

'Still-waking sleep, that is not what it is' (Act 1 scene 1)
'Bid a sick man in sadness make his will?' (Act 1 scene 1)
'Shut up in prison, kept without my food' (Act 1 scene 2)
'Then "banished" / Is death, mis-term'd' (Act 3 scene 3)
'O mischief thou art swift / To enter in the thoughts of desperate men!' (Act 5 scene 1)

Metaphor
Oxymoron
Personification
Rhetorical question
Hyperbole

Revise 2

Explain how Romeo's inner turmoil relating to his punishment is shown in the following quotations from Act 3 scene 3.

a)

> What sorrow craves acquaintance at my hand
>
> That I yet know not?

b)

> Hadst thou no poison mix'd, no sharp-ground knife,
>
> No sudden mean of death, though ne'er so mean,
>
> But 'banished' to kill me?

c)

> Thou canst not speak of that thou dost not feel.

Write two paragraphs analysing how Shakespeare conveys Juliet's inner turmoil in Act 4 scene 1. Where relevant, link your ideas to the play's context.

....

....

....

....

....

....

....

....

Look at this scene from Act 3 and fill in the missing key quotation.

THERE'S NO TRUST, NO FAITH, NO HONESTY IN MEN.

Extend

Thinking about your response to the Revise 3 task, how is Juliet's inner turmoil developed further in Act 4 scene 3? Write two or three paragraphs, linking your ideas to the play's context.

Active Learning

Create a learning poster on the theme of inner turmoil and its causes, including clear references to characters, key scenes and useful quotations.

Revise 1

The Capulet and Montague families can be described as *traditional* and *patriarchal*. What do these two words mean? Supporting your answer with quotations, explain why these words are appropriate.

Revise 2

Explain how the following quotations suggest that the Montague and Capulet parents set a bad example for their children. How might each quotation link to the children's later actions?

a)

LORD CAPULET:	My sword I say! Old Montague is come,
	And flourishes his blade in spite of me.
LORD MONTAGUE:	Thou villain Capulet! Hold me not! Let me go! (Act 1 scene 1)

b)

LADY CAPULET:	Well, think of marriage now …
	Read o'er the volume of young Paris's face
	And find delight writ there with beauty's pen. (Act 1 scene 3)

Writing one paragraph about the Montagues and one about the Capulets, analyse how Shakespeare conveys the parents' love for their children. Where relevant, link your ideas to the play's context.

....

....

....

....

....

....

....

....

....

....

Look at this scene from Act 3 and fill in the missing key quotation.

GOD IN HEAVEN BLESS HER!
YOU ARE TO BLAME, MY LORD, TO RATE HER SO.

OUT ON HER, HILDING.

Extend

Thinking about your response to the Revise 3 task, write two or three paragraphs exploring how Shakespeare also presents a distance between the parents and their children. Link your ideas to the play's context.

Active Learning

Using illustrations and quotations, create a diagram showing how Lord Capulet and Lord Montague rely on other characters to act as go-betweens with their children. Consider also the role of Friar Laurence in their family lives.

Themes

Fate

Revise 1

What is *fate* and how is the idea established in the play's prologue? Use quotations to support your answer.

....

....

....

....

....

Revise 2

Explain what the following quotations suggest the characters feel about the role fate has in their lives.

a)

| ROMEO: O, I am fortune's fool. (Act 3 scene 1) |

....

....

....

b)

| JULIET: O Fortune, Fortune! All men call thee fickle. (Act 3 scene 5) |

....

....

....

c)

| ROMEO: Then I defy you, stars! (Act 5 scene 1) |

....

....

....

Look at the start of Act 3 scene 5 (up to Romeo's exit, 'Adieu, adieu'). Write two paragraphs analysing how Shakespeare foreshadows the tragedies of Act 5 scene 3, implying the role of fate in the play's events.

....

....

....

....

....

....

....

....

....

....

Look at this scene from Act 5 and fill in the missing key quotation.

I'LL BURY THEE IN A TRIUMPHANT GRAVE; A GRAVE? O NO! A LANTERN, SLAUGHTER'D YOUTH.

Extend

Thinking about your response to the Revise 3 task, where else does Shakespeare foreshadow different events in the play? You might consider Act 1 scene 4, Act 2 scene 4, Act 3 scene 2 and Act 5 scene 1.

Active Learning

Using illustrations and quotations, create a diagram showing the interlinking events leading up to the deaths of Romeo and Juliet. Consider how Shakespeare structures his narrative to suggest his characters are victims of fate.

Revise 1

Suggest two parts of the play in which characters are rushed by others, and two parts of the play where decisions or events are mistimed. Support each suggestion with a quotation.

....

....

....

....

....

....

Revise 2

Find and explain quotations that suggest the following characters died too soon:

a) Mercutio

....

....

....

b) Juliet (after she fakes her death)

....

....

....

c) Paris and Romeo

....

....

....

Focus on either Act 3 scene 4 or Act 4 scene 1. Write two paragraphs analysing how Shakespeare creates a sense of urgency, increasing the pace of the play as it moves towards its tragic climax.

....

....

....

....

....

....

....

....

....

....

Look at this scene from Act 5 and fill in the missing key quotation.

ROMEO! O, PALE! WHO ELSE?
WHAT, PARIS TOO?
AND STEEP'D IN BLOOD?

Extend

Looking at Act 5, write two or three paragraphs exploring how Shakespeare uses language and the structure of the play to suggest that Romeo and Juliet are victims of time.

Active Learning

Using illustrations and quotations, create a timeline of events to show how quickly things happen in the play.

Read the following extract from Act 1 scene 5 and then answer the question that follows.

At this point in the play, Tybalt realises that Romeo has come uninvited to the Capulet party.

TYBALT:	This, by his voice, should be a Montague.
	Fetch me my rapier, boy. What, dares the slave
	Come hither, cover'd with an antic face,
	To fleer and scorn at our solemnity?
	Now, by the stock and honour of my kin,
	To strike him dead, I hold it not a sin.
CAPULET:	Why, how now, kinsman! wherefore storm you so?
TYBALT:	Uncle, this is a Montague, our foe:
	A villain that is hither come in spite,
	To scorn at our solemnity this night.
CAPULET:	Young Romeo is it?
TYBALT:	'Tis he, that villain Romeo.
CAPULET:	Content thee, gentle coz, let him alone,
	He bears him like a portly gentleman;
	And, to say truth, Verona brags of him
	To be a virtuous and well-govern'd youth.
	I would not for the wealth of all the town
	Here in my house do him disparagement.
	Therefore be patient, take no note of him.
	It is my will, the which if thou respect,
	Show a fair presence and put off these frowns,
	An ill-beseeming semblance for a feast.
TYBALT:	It fits when such a villain is a guest:
	I'll not endure him.

Starting with this extract, explore how Shakespeare presents Tybalt as aggressive. Write about:

- how Shakespeare presents Tybalt's aggression in this extract
- how Shakespeare presents Tybalt's aggression in the play as a whole.

 Revise 1

Underline the words or phrases that show what you need to focus on to successfully answer the question.

Plan your response to the question: annotate the extract, add notes about elsewhere in the play, and then come up with four to six ideas, linked to quotations and contextual references.

Write an introduction to your answer, giving a clear overview of the question and your approach to it. Then write up your first point. Spend a maximum of 15 minutes on this task.

Extend

Finish off your response to the question, using the time you have remaining from the allocated 50 minutes.

Read the following extract from Act 4 scene 2 and then answer the question that follows.

At this point in the play, Juliet returns from Friar Laurence and pretends to be willing to marry Paris.

CAPULET:	What, is my daughter gone to Friar Laurence?
NURSE:	Ay, forsooth.
CAPULET:	Well, he may chance to do some good on her.
	A peevish self-will'd harlotry it is.
NURSE:	See where she comes from shrift with merry look. [*Enter JULIET*]
CAPULET:	How now, my headstrong! where have you been gadding?
JULIET:	Where I have learn'd me to repent the sin
	Of disobedient opposition
	To you and your behests, and am enjoin'd
	By holy Laurence to fall prostrate here,
	To beg your pardon. Pardon, I beseech you!
	Henceforward I am ever rul'd by you. [*She kneels down*]
CAPULET:	Send for the County; go tell him of this.
	I'll have this knot knit up tomorrow morning.
JULIET:	I met the youthful lord at Laurence's cell,
	And gave him what becomed love I might,
	Not stepping o'er the bounds of modesty.
CAPULET:	Why, I am glad on't. This is well. Stand up.
	This is as't should be. Let me see the County.
	Ay, marry. Go, I say, and fetch him hither.
	Now, afore God, this reverend holy Friar,
	Our whole city is much bound to him.

Starting with this extract, explore how Shakespeare presents the relationship between Lord Capulet and Juliet. Write about:

- how Shakespeare presents their relationship in this extract
- how Shakespeare presents their relationship in the play as a whole.

> **Revise 1**

Underline the words or phrases that show what you need to focus on to successfully answer the question.

Plan your response to the question: annotate the extract, add notes about elsewhere in the play, and then come up with four to six ideas, linked to quotations and contextual references.

Write an introduction to your answer, giving a clear overview of the question and your approach to it. Then write up your first point. Spend a maximum of 15 minutes on this task.

Finish off your response to the question, using the time you have remaining from the allocated 50 minutes.

Read the following extract from Act 2 scene 5 and then answer the question that follows.

At this point in the play, Juliet is waiting for the Nurse to tell her Romeo's message.

NURSE:	Your love says, like an honest gentleman,
	And a courteous, and a kind, and a handsome,
	And I warrant a virtuous, – Where is your mother?
JULIET:	Where is my mother? Why, she is within.
	Where should she be? How oddly thou repliest!
	'Your love says, like an honest gentleman,
	"Where is your mother?"'
NURSE:	O God's lady dear,
	Are you so hot? Marry, come up, I trow.
	Is this the poultice for my aching bones?
	Henceforward do your messages yourself.
JULIET:	Here's such a coil. Come, what says Romeo?
NURSE:	Have you got leave to go to shrift today?
JULIET:	I have.
NURSE:	Then hie you hence to Friar Laurence's cell.
	There stays a husband to make you a wife.
	Now comes the wanton blood up in your cheeks.
	They'll be in scarlet straight at any news.
	Hie you to church. I must another way,
	To fetch a ladder by the which your love
	Must climb a bird's nest soon when it is dark.
	I am the drudge, and toil in your delight,
	But you shall bear the burden soon at night.

Starting with this extract, explore how Shakespeare presents the Nurse. Write about:

- how Shakespeare presents the Nurse in this extract
- how Shakespeare presents the Nurse in the play as a whole.

Revise 1

Underline the words or phrases that show what you need to focus on to successfully answer the question.

Plan your response to the question: annotate the extract, add notes about elsewhere in the play, and then come up with four to six ideas, linked to quotations and contextual references.

Write an introduction to your answer, giving a clear overview of the question and your approach to it. Then write up your first point. Spend a maximum of 15 minutes on this task.

Finish off your response to the question, using the time you have remaining from the allocated 50 minutes.

Read the following extract from Act 1 scene 5 and then answer the question that follows.

At this point in the play, Romeo and Juliet meet for the first time.

ROMEO:	If I profane with my unworthiest hand
	This holy shrine, the gentle fine is this:
	My lips, two blushing pilgrims, ready stand
	To smooth that rough touch with a tender kiss.
JULIET:	Good pilgrim, you do wrong your hand too much,
	Which mannerly devotion shows in this;
	For saints have hands that pilgrims' hands do touch,
	And palm to palm is holy palmers' kiss.
ROMEO:	Have not saints lips, and holy palmers too?
JULIET:	Ay, pilgrim, lips that they must use in prayer.
ROMEO:	O then, dear saint, let lips do what hands do:
	They pray: grant thou, lest faith turn to despair.
JULIET:	Saints do not move, though grant for prayers' sake.
ROMEO:	Then move not, while my prayer's effect I take. [*He kisses her*]
	Thus from my lips, by thine, my sin is purg'd.
JULIET:	Then have my lips the sin that they have took.
ROMEO:	Sin from thy lips? O trespass sweetly urg'd.
	Give me my sin again. [*He kisses her*]
JULIET:	You kiss by the book.
NURSE:	Madam, your mother craves a word with you.

Starting with this extract, explore how Shakespeare presents love in the play. Write about:

- how Shakespeare presents love in this extract
- how Shakespeare presents love in the play as a whole.

 Revise 1 >

Underline the words or phrases that show what you need to focus on to successfully answer the question.

Plan your response to the question: annotate the extract, add notes about elsewhere in the play, and then come up with four to six ideas, linked to quotations and contextual references.

Write an introduction to your answer, giving a clear overview of the question and your approach to it. Then write up your first point. Spend a maximum of 15 minutes on this task.

Extend

Finish off your response to the question, using the time you have remaining from the allocated 50 minutes.

Read the following extract from Act 3 scene 1 and then answer the question that follows.

At this point in the play, Mercutio has been stabbed and Tybalt has fled.

MERCUTIO:	A plague o' both your houses,
	They have made worms' meat of me. I have it,
	And soundly too. Your houses! [*Exit MERCUTIO with BENVOLIO*]
ROMEO:	This gentleman, the Prince's near ally,
	My very friend, hath got his mortal hurt
	In my behalf – my reputation stain'd
	With Tybalt's slander – Tybalt that an hour
	Hath been my cousin. O sweet Juliet,
	Thy beauty hath made me effeminate
	And in my temper soften'd valour's steel. [*Enter BENVOLIO*]
BENVOLIO:	O Romeo, Romeo, brave Mercutio's dead!
	That gallant spirit hath aspir'd the clouds
	Which too untimely here did scorn the earth.
ROMEO:	This day's black fate on more days doth depend:
	This but begins the woe, others must end. [*Enter TYBALT*]
BENVOLIO:	Here comes the furious Tybalt back again.
ROMEO:	Alive, in triumph! and Mercutio slain!
	Away to heaven, respective lenity,
	And fire-ey'd fury be my conduct now!
	Now, Tybalt, take the villain back again
	That late thou gav'st me; for Mercutio's soul
	Is but a little way above our heads,
	Staying for thine to keep him company.
	Either thou, or I, or both, must go with him.

Starting with this extract, explore how Shakespeare presents death in the play. Write about:

- how Shakespeare presents death in this extract
- how Shakespeare presents death in the play as a whole.

> **Revise 1**
>
> Underline the words or phrases that show what you need to focus on to successfully answer the question.

Plan your response to the question: annotate the extract, add notes about elsewhere in the play, and then come up with four to six ideas, linked to quotations and contextual references.

Write an introduction to your answer, giving a clear overview of the question and your approach to it. Then write up your first point. Spend a maximum of 15 minutes on this task.

Finish off your response to the question, using the time you have remaining from the allocated 50 minutes.

Read the following extract from Act 1 scene 3 and then answer the question that follows.

At this point in the play, Lady Capulet, the Nurse and Juliet are discussing love and marriage.

NURSE:	Thou wast the prettiest babe that e'er I nurs'd.
	And I might live to see thee married once,
	I have my wish.
LADY CAPULET:	Marry, that 'marry' is the very theme
	I came to talk of. Tell me, daughter Juliet,
	How stands your disposition to be married?
JULIET:	It is an honour that I dream not of.
NURSE:	An honour! Were not I thine only nurse,
	I would say thou hadst suck'd wisdom from thy teat.
LADY CAPULET:	Well, think of marriage now. Younger than you,
	Here in Verona, ladies of esteem,
	Are made already mothers. By my count,
	I was your mother much upon these years
	That you are now a maid. Thus then in brief:
	The valiant Paris seeks you for his love.
NURSE:	A man, young lady! Lady, such a man
	As all the world – why, he's a man of wax.
LADY CAPULET:	Verona's summer hath not such a flower.
NURSE:	Nay, he's a flower, in faith a very flower.
LADY CAPULET:	What say you? Can you love the gentleman?

Starting with this extract, explore how Shakespeare presents attitudes to marriage in the play. Write about:

- how Shakespeare presents attitudes to marriage in this extract
- how Shakespeare presents attitudes to marriage in the play as a whole.

Revise 1

Underline the words or phrases that show what you need to focus on to successfully answer the question.

Plan your response to the question: annotate the extract, add notes about elsewhere in the play, and then come up with four to six ideas, linked to quotations and contextual references.

Write an introduction to your answer, giving a clear overview of the question and your approach to it. Then write up your first point. Spend a maximum of 15 minutes on this task.

....

....

....

....

....

....

....

....

....

....

....

....

Extend

Finish off your response to the question, using the time you have remaining from the allocated 50 minutes.

Read the following extract from Act 4 scene 3 and then answer the question that follows.

At this point in the play, Juliet is preparing to take the potion that will fake her death.

> JULIET: There's a fearful point!
>
> Shall I not, then, be stifled in the vault,
>
> To whose foul mouth no healthsome air breathes in,
>
> And there die strangled ere my Romeo comes?
>
> Or, if I live, is it not very like,
>
> The horrible conceit of death and night,
>
> Together with the terror of the place,
>
> As in a vault, an ancient receptacle,
>
> Where, for these many hundred years, the bones
>
> Of all my buried ancestors are pack'd,
>
> Where bloody Tybalt, yet but green in earth,
>
> Lies festering in his shroud; where, as they say,
>
> At some hours in the night spirits resort –
>
> Alack, alack! Is it not like that I,
>
> So early waking, what with loathsome smells,
>
> And shrieks like mandrakes torn out of the earth,
>
> That living mortals, hearing them, run mad –
>
> O, if I wake, shall I not be distraught,
>
> Environed with all these hideous fears?
>
> And madly play with my forefathers' joints?
>
> And pluck the mangled Tybalt from his shroud?
>
> And, in this rage, with some great kinsman's bone
>
> As with a club, dash out my desperate brains?

Starting with this extract, explore how Shakespeare presents inner turmoil in the play. Write about:

- how Shakespeare presents inner turmoil in this extract
- how Shakespeare presents inner turmoil in the play as a whole.

> **Revise 1**
>
> Underline the words or phrases that show what you need to focus on to successfully answer the question.

Plan your response to the question: annotate the extract, add notes about elsewhere in the play, and then come up with four to six ideas, linked to quotations and contextual references.

Write an introduction to your answer, giving a clear overview of the question and your approach to it. Then write up your first point. Spend a maximum of 15 minutes on this task.

Finish off your response to the question, using the time you have remaining from the allocated 50 minutes.

Answers

Pages 4–5

Revise 1

1. A sonnet summarises the events of the play, creating a sense of fate and tragedy.
2. A fight between the Capulets and the Montagues is stopped by Prince Escalus.
3. Lord and Lady Montague are worried about their son, Romeo; he reveals to his friend, Benvolio, that he is suffering from unrequited love for a girl called Rosaline.
4. Lord Capulet and Paris discuss Paris's wish to marry Juliet; Capulet feels his daughter is too young to get married.

Revise 2

Answers might include: 'Ay me! sad hours seem long' – adjectives showing his unhappiness as he yearns for Rosaline's love; 'Feather of lead, bright smoke, cold fire, sick health!' and other oxymorons show his inner turmoil due to unrequited love; 'Griefs of mine own lie heavy in my breast' – metaphor for the pain of unrequited love; 'a madness most discreet, / A choking gall, and a preserving sweet' – pattern of three metaphors to show that unrequited love is obsessive, oppressive and addictive; 'she'll not be hit / With Cupid's arrow' – classical allusion to show his love and frustration; 'in that vow / Do I live dead …' – oxymoron showing the pain and desperation of unrequited love.

Revise 3

Answers might include: 'My child is yet a stranger in the world' – metaphor to suggest Juliet is too young and inexperienced for marriage; 'The earth hath swallow'd all my hopes but she; / She is the hopeful lady of my earth' – the metaphor explains that Lord Capulet's other children are dead so Juliet is even more precious to him, perhaps linking to ideas of inheritance; 'My will to her consent is but a part' – unusually for the time, Lord Capulet implies that who Juliet marries is ultimately her choice; however, he still objectifies her in the metaphor 'ripe to be a bride' as higher-class marriages were linked to social and financial advancement.

Extend

Answers might explore: the family conflict is established in the prologue alongside the foreshadowing of its consequences ('From forth the fatal loins of these two foes'), linking to Elizabethan beliefs in fate; the physical conflict between the Montagues and the Capulets ('Rebellious subjects, enemies to peace') is portrayed in Act 1 scene 1, possibly relating to the Wars of the Roses or Elizabethan riots; there is conflict between family members as Lady Montague tries to restrain her husband ('Thou shalt not stir one foot to seek a foe'); Romeo's internal conflict, caused by unrequited love ('O anything of nothing first create!'), is introduced; there is conflict of values in Act 1 scene 2 as Lord Capulet resists Paris's wish to marry Juliet ('And too soon marr'd are those so early made').

Comic Strip

'I hate the word, / As I hate hell, all Montagues, and thee.'

Pages 6–7

Revise 1

1. Lady Capulet encourages Juliet to think about getting married.
2. As soon as he sees Juliet at the Capulets' feast, Romeo falls in love with her.
3. Tybalt is angry that Romeo is at the feast; he wants to fight him but is stopped by Lord Capulet.
4. Romeo and Juliet talk and kiss. Once they have parted, they realise that each is from their rival family.

Revise 2

Answers should include: a) the metaphor shows his love and appreciation for Juliet's beauty (with fire also symbolising passion), emphasised by the alliteration; b) rhetorical question to suggest that this new love surpasses all others (and that he has now forgotten Rosaline) and amazement at Juliet's beauty; c) rhetorical question suggesting a mix of shock and despair at Juliet's family, which is emphasised by the money metaphor (suggesting he is now forever in debt to the Capulets for bringing him Juliet, but that he'll never be able to pay that debt and gain Juliet's love because the family won't accept him).

Revise 3

Answers might include: the imperative 'Well, think of marriage now' shows her urging Juliet to marry; unlike Lord Capulet's protectiveness and reasoning in Act 1 scene 2, she bases her ideas on personal experience ('I was your mother much upon these years') and social expectations ('younger than you / Here in Verona, ladies of esteem, / Are made already mothers'), with the noun 'esteem' linking to how marriage was seen as a way to increase status; the idea of gaining status through marriage is returned to in the 'precious book of love' extended metaphor; adjectives ('valiant') and metaphor ('such a flower') are used to present Paris as worth marrying.

Extend

Answers might explore: the repeated use of religious imagery ('holy shrine … blushing pilgrims') places their love in the context of the Catholic setting whilst implying that their love is pure and honourable; their love is both sensual (the verbs, nouns and adjectives in 'smooth that rough touch with a tender kiss') and respectful ('If I profane'); their love is also equal, with Juliet's language being similar to Romeo's ('palm to palm is holy palmers' kiss') and the two characters sharing the lines and rhymes of the sonnet as well as its imagery; the relationship is consensual (for example, the repetition of 'grant' rather than arranged.

Comic Strip

'Go ask his name. If he be married, / My grave is like to be my wedding bed.'

Pages 8–9

Revise 1

1. Romeo returns to the Capulet house and watches Juliet on her balcony.
2. Juliet talks of her wish that Romeo wasn't a Montague.
3. Romeo and Juliet say they love each other; she suggests they marry the next day.
4. Friar Laurence agrees to join the two lovers in marriage.

Revise 2

Answers should include: he is worried that Romeo's love is too fickle or temporary (for example, using a rhetorical question and metaphor to comment on Romeo's previous love for Rosaline: 'Is Rosaline … / So soon forsaken? Young men's love then lies / Not truly in their hearts but in their eyes.'); he expresses hope that Romeo and Juliet's love can bring the two warring families together (for example, using contrasting abstract nouns: 'To turn your households' rancour to pure love'); he is worried that Romeo is rushing into a dangerous situation (the proverb, 'Wisely and slow; they stumble that run fast').

Revise 3

Answers might include: Romeo uses metaphor ('Juliet is the sun') to suggest her beauty and to convey the passion he feels, making her seem almost like a goddess; he uses celestial images (such as comparing her eyes to 'Two of the fairest stars in all the heaven' or calling her 'bright angel') to convey her beauty and purity (linking to expectations of girls' purity and the religious context), and perhaps to suggest that his love feels special and unique; the repeated reference to 'stars' also links to the play's theme of fate; once they speak to each other, personification is used to convey the power of Romeo's love ('love's light wings'); he is worried that his love is unrequited (the metaphor 'there lies more peril in thine eye / Than twenty of their swords'); Juliet says that she would give up her family name ('I'll no longer be a Capulet'), which would be a big sacrifice for a girl from a wealthy family; she can see past his surname ('That which we call a rose / By any other name would smell as sweet') and Romeo mirrors this feeling (saying to himself that he would be 'new baptis'd'); Juliet asks Romeo to 'pronounce it [his love] faithfully' and refers to 'My true love's passion'; she uses metaphor ('This bud of love, by summer's ripening breath, / May prove a beauteous flower when next we meet') to convey her commitment and her hope that their love will develop and strengthen; she uses simile ('My bounty is as boundless as the sea, / My love as deep') to convey the strength of her love; it is Juliet who suggests marriage ('wilt perform the rite; / And all my fortunes at thy foot I'll lay') and pledges her commitment to him.

Extend

Answers might explore: several phrases in Act 2 scene 2 link with the theme of fate, continuing the ideas from the prologue that they are 'star-cross'd'; as well as the references to 'stars', Romeo uses personification to suggest that 'love' led him to Juliet ('I am no pilot, yet wert thou as far …'); Juliet refers to the classical gods ('Jove'), alluding to how they were believed to manipulate the lives of mortals. Shakespeare also includes several references to death to foreshadow the consequences of their love (another key idea established by the prologue); Juliet describes the danger Romeo is in by coming to her balcony ('the place death … they will murder thee'); she refers to the story of Echo who died from unrequited love and she describes how she would 'kill thee with much cherishing'.

Comic Strip

'That which we call a rose / By any other name would smell as sweet.'

Pages 10–11
Revise 1

1. Romeo jokes with his friends, Mercutio and Benvolio, but doesn't tell them about Juliet.
2. Romeo asks the Nurse to pass on a message to Juliet, confirming their marriage later that day.
3. Juliet anxiously awaits a message from Romeo which the Nurse eventually gives her.
4. Romeo and Juliet meet with Friar Laurence to be married.

Revise 2

Answers should include: the opening phrase 'Alas, poor Romeo' suggests Romeo's sadness at his unrequited love; this is developed by the extended death metaphor, conveying the pain Romeo feels and suggesting that it's ruining his life; however, the hyperbole in these images creates a tone of mockery, suggesting Romeo is seen by Mercutio as foolish for falling in love; the references to a 'love song' and Cupid ('blind bow-boy') present Romeo as romantic and gentle; this gentleness is emphasised by the rhetorical question, suggesting he is different (less manly and aggressive) from Tybalt.

Revise 3

Answers might include: Juliet trusts the Nurse (the verb 'promis'd'); there is affection between them (the adjectives in 'honey nurse' and 'sweet nurse'), with their strong bond linking to how a nurse would breastfeed and raise the child of a wealthy family; but the Nurse is mischievous and enjoys exasperating Juliet (constantly diverting the conversation away from Romeo's message: '… and, I warrant, a virtuous – Where is your mother?'), linking to her role as a comic character as well as showing an unusual relationship for a wealthy girl and the family's servant; their closeness is also shown in the way the Nurse is actually excited by, and encourages, the marriage with Romeo (the imperative 'Hie you to church'); their strong bond, despite their class differences, is also shown through the way the Nurse is free to be angry with

Juliet ('Are you so hot?') and to make, considering her position as a servant and Juliet's age, inappropriate sexual innuendos ('you shall bear the burden soon at night').

Extend

Answers might explore: the adverb in the Friar's warning, 'Therefore love moderately', links back to his previous suggestion in Act 2 scene 3 that Romeo is too impulsive; the simile 'like fire and powder' relates to explosions and suggests their sudden passion is dangerous; the stage direction *Juliet somewhat fast* creates a physical image of the relationship being rushed; the key scene that suggests the relationship is being rushed is Act 2 scene 2 with its many references to time (night, morning, moon, tomorrow, o'clock, Titan's wheels), Juliet worrying about the relationship developing too quickly (the list and the simile 'It is too rash, too unadvised, too sudden; / Too like the lightning') and her sudden suggestion of marriage; a tone of urgency is also created through the Nurse calling for Juliet, as Romeo is in danger of being discovered and must leave; other relevant scenes include the Nurse seeming surprised that the wedding is so soon ('This afternoon, sir?' II iv) and Juliet urging the Nurse to pass on Romeo's message (II v).

Comic Strip

'Then love-devouring death do what he dare: / It is enough I may but call her mine.'

Pages 12–13
Revise 1

1. A group of Montagues and Capulets meet; Tybalt and Mercutio begin to argue.
2. Romeo arrives but refuses to fight Tybalt so Mercutio fights him instead.
3. Romeo tries to stop the fight, resulting in Mercutio being stabbed by Tybalt. In revenge, Romeo kills Tybalt.
4. Prince Escalus pronounces Romeo's banishment from Verona.

Revise 2

Answers should include: a) Romeo tries to convince Tybalt that they need not be enemies (the verb 'protest'), saying he's done him no wrong (the verb 'injured') and making a veiled reference to his marriage to Juliet (the dramatic irony of 'love thee better than thou canst devise'); b) After Mercutio's death, Romeo's anger and hatred of Tybalt (the metaphor 'fire-ey'd fury') replaces his previous attitude of restraint ('Away … lenity'); c) Romeo wants to kill Tybalt to avenge Mercutio's death ('thou … must go with him'); his hatred combines with his own guilt and makes him ready to fight Tybalt to the death ('thou, or I').

Revise 3

Answers might include: her speech focuses on the idea that she has misjudged Romeo and that he has tricked her ('deceit'), now believing that his outward appearance hid his evil character (summarised in the line 'Just opposite to what thou justly seem'st'); the opening metaphor and contrasting imagery establish this idea, possibly drawing on Christian imagery of the Garden of Eden;

it is continued in her subsequent rhetorical question (contrasting 'dragon' and 'fair'), and then the list of oxymorons ('fiend angelical, / Dove-feather'd raven'); as in their initial dialogue in Act 1 scene 4, religious imagery is used but now links to evil ('damned saint … hell'); she also refers back to her dialogue with Lady Capulet about Paris in Act 1 scene 3 (the rhetorical question and metaphor 'Was ever book containing such vile matter / So fairly bound?').

Extend

Answers might explore: Juliet's speech is full of rhetorical questions to show her confusion; her words show that she feels caught between her family loyalty and the loyalty to her wedding vows, both of which would arguably have had a stronger impact on her behaviour in the context of the play than they might have today; she uses metaphor to show her feelings of guilt for having thought badly of Romeo ('Ah, poor my lord, what tongue shall smooth thy name / When I, thy three-hours wife, have mangled it?'); words like 'lord' and 'husband' are contrasted with 'villain' to show her conflicting feelings, and this is developed when she refers to Tybalt as 'cousin' and then 'villain cousin' to convey her mixed loyalties; Juliet also talks of contrasting feelings of 'joy' (that Romeo was not killed) and 'woe' (that Tybalt is dead); she acknowledges that, while she grieves for Tybalt's death, she is more upset ('worser than Tybalt's death') by the news of Romeo's banishment (conveyed through the hyperbole of 'that one word "banished" / Hath slain ten thousand Tybalts', and emphasised by the list, 'There is no end, no limit, measure, bound, / In that word's death.').

Comic Strip

'A plague o' both your houses.'

Pages 14–15
Revise 1

1. Friar Laurence brings news to Romeo that he has been banished from Verona.
2. Lord Capulet decides that Juliet should marry Paris in three days' time.
3. Romeo and Juliet spend their wedding night together and reluctantly part in the morning.
4. Juliet angers her parents by refusing to marry Paris; the Nurse advises her to forget Romeo.

Revise 2

Answers should include: a) even though banishment seems better than being executed ('golden axe … smilest'), the extended death metaphor shows that Romeo feels it is worse because he cannot live without Juliet; b) he continues to describe how banishment ('torture') is worse than execution because he'll be without Juliet (the 'heaven' metaphor) so it will be a living hell; c) he doesn't want the Friar to keep trying to comfort him ('talk no more') as he is full of despair at the news of his banishment and thinks nothing can help him.

Revise 3

Answers might include: at first, Lord Capulet doesn't believe what he has heard (the repetition of 'take me with you' and the series of questions such as 'will she none?'); he is angry at what he sees as Juliet's ingratitude for her upbringing and the arranged marriage, linking to the position of women in society and the idea of marriage as a means to increase status ('doth she not count her blest, / Unworthy as she is, that we have wrought / So worthy a gentleman to be her bridegroom?'); his anger rises as he mimics Juliet ('What is this? / "Proud" and "I thank you"') and insults her ('mistress minion … green-sickness carrion … baggage!'); linking to the idea that girls were their father's property ('And you be mine, I'll give you to my friend'), he threatens to force her to marry ('I will drag thee on a hurdle thither'); linking to the vulnerable position of women in society, Lord Capulet threatens to disown her (the imperative 'Get thee to church o' Thursday, / Or never after look me in the face' and the short commands 'Beg! Starve! Die in the streets!' with exclamation marks implying the actor should be shouting); he is tempted to hit her ('My fingers itch') and, linking to the religious setting, describes her as a 'curse'.

Extend

Answers might explore: linking to the superior status of the husband as head of the household, Lady Capulet immediately defers to Lord Capulet ('Here comes your father; tell him so yourself'); like Lord Capulet, she wishes her daughter dead ('I would the fool were married to her grave') which is an example of dramatic irony, as the audience knows Juliet's fate from the prologue; despite Juliet's desperation and unhappiness, Lady Capulet shows no sympathy for her daughter ('Talk not to me'), perhaps, linking to Act 1 scene 3, because she believes that marriage is all about status; like Lord Capulet, she speaks as if she is disowning Juliet ('I have done with thee').

Comic Strip

'We will have vengeance for it, fear thou not.'

Pages 16–17

Revise 1

1. Friar Laurence outlines his plan for Juliet to fake her death so Romeo can collect her and take her back to Mantua.
2. Juliet apologises to her father for her disobedience.
3. Lord Capulet brings forward the marriage by a day and Juliet takes the Friar's potion.
4. Juliet is found, apparently dead, by the Nurse; her parents are distraught.

Revise 2

Answers might include: 'I have a faint cold fear thrills through my veins … My dismal scene I needs must act alone' shows her fear, desperation and loneliness; the rhetorical questions 'What if this mixture do not work at all? / Shall I be married then tomorrow morning?' show she is worried that the potion won't work and she'll have to marry Paris; 'this shall forbid it: lie thou there. [Laying down her dagger]' indicates that she plans to kill herself if the potion does not work; 'Subtly hath minister'd to have me dead / Lest in this marriage he should be

dishonour'd' suggests she is paranoid that Friar Laurence is trying to kill her to hide his involvement; 'And there die strangled ere my Romeo comes' indicates she is scared that she will die in the vault before Romeo arrives; the personification 'Shall I not, then, be stifled in the vault, / To whose foul mouth no wholesome air breathes in …?' shows she is afraid she will die of suffocation in the tomb; while 'what with loathsome smells, / And shrieks like mandrakes torn out of the earth, / That living mortals, hearing them, run mad' indicates her fear that the tomb will make her mad and that she may kill herself as a result ('dash out my desperate brains?').

Revise 3

Answers might include: Lady Capulet is distraught and suggests the grief will kill her (repetition and metaphor, 'O me, O me! My child, my only life!', and the pattern of three, 'Revive, look up, or I will die with thee!'); her grief is reinforced by exclamative sentences and patterns of three ('Alack the day! She's dead, she's dead, she's dead! … O woeful time!'); adjectives convey her unhappiness ('Accurs'd, unhappy, wretched, hateful day! / Most miserable hour that e'er time saw'); linking to the Catholic context and popular superstition, death is personified to suggest Lady Capulet almost feels punished ('But one thing to rejoice and solace in, / And cruel Death hath catch'd it from my sight.'); Lord Capulet is equally shocked but Shakespeare gives him a more poetic response; he loved Juliet and feels she has died too young (the simile, 'Death lies on her like an untimely frost / Upon the sweetest flower of all the field.'); like his wife, he also sees Death as punishing him and finds it difficult to express his grief ('Death, that hath ta'en her hence to make me wail, / Ties up my tongue and will not let me speak'); he shows sympathy for Paris's loss but also conveys his sadness that he will have no heir, linking to the importance of inheritance to wealthy, established families ('O son, the night before thy wedding day / Hath death lain with thy bride … / Death is my son-in-law, Death is my heir'); he feels Juliet was everything to him ('O child! O child! My soul, and not my child') and he will never be happy again ('And with my child my joys are buried!').

Extend

Answers might explore: the contrasting cruelty shown by Lord and Lady Capulet towards Juliet earlier and the grief displayed now (see answers to the Revise 3 and Extend tasks for pages 14–15 and the Revise 3 answer above); although the Nurse tried to support Juliet in Act 3 scene 5 ('God in heaven bless her! / You are to blame, my lord, to rate her so.'), Capulet's fury and her own pragmatic outlook on life did lead her to suggest forgetting Romeo ('Romeo is banish'd … I think it best you married with the County') which made Juliet feel let down; in Act 4 scene 5, the Nurse's response is much more emotional (the repetition and exclamative sentences in 'O lamentable day!', 'She's dead, deceas'd, she's dead; alack the day!' and 'O woe! O woeful, woeful, woeful day!').

Comic Strip

'Death, that hath ta'en her hence to make me wail / Ties up my tongue, and will not let me speak.'

Pages 18–19

Revise 1

1. Romeo is brought news of Juliet's death; knowing nothing of Friar Laurence's plan, he buys poison and makes his way to Juliet's tomb.
2. Romeo and Paris fight outside Juliet's tomb and Paris is killed.
3. Romeo lays down by Juliet and drinks the poison; waking, Juliet finds Romeo dead and stabs herself.
4. At the sight of their dead children, Lord Capulet and Lord Montague are reconciled.

Revise 2

Answers should include: 'flattering truth' and 'presage some joyful news' show that Romeo hopes his dream means he will see Juliet again soon; the personification of the heart ('My bosom's lord sits lightly in his throne') suggests he is excited about their reunion; hope is also conveyed through the metaphor 'lifts me above', showing his spirits have been raised, and the reference to 'cheerful thoughts'; thinking of being reunited with his lover ('kisses … how sweet is love') makes him feel happier ('breath'd such life', 'reviv'd', 'rich in joy!'); the image of an 'emperor' suggests that seeing Juliet again will make him feel happier than ever before; however, the dream also foreshadows his death: 'my lady came and found me dead', linking to the idea that this is his fate and it cannot be avoided.

Revise 3

Answers should include: Romeo's love and grief is shown through how he describes Juliet, using traditional references to female beauty; metaphor suggests that, even though she is dead, her beauty is powerful enough to light the whole tomb ('and her beauty makes / This vault a feasting presence, full of light.'); he laments the death of Juliet but reiterates her beauty (using personification that matches the Catholic context and superstition at the time: 'O my love! my wife! / Death, that hath suck'd the honey of thy breath / Hath had no power yet upon thy beauty.'); this idea is repeated through personification ('beauty's ensign yet / Is crimson in thy lips and in thy cheeks, / And Death's pale flag is not advanced there.'); the rhetorical question, 'Ah, dear Juliet, / Why art thou yet so fair?', suggests that her beauty increases his sadness because it emphasises what he has lost.

Extend

Answers might explore: the Prince's opening words ('What misadventure is so early up …') mirror line 7 of the Prologue, reminding the audience that Romeo and Juliet were tragically fated to die; he later blames their deaths on the family conflict (using an imperative to highlight the angry tone of the metaphor 'See, what a scourge is laid upon your hate, / That heaven finds means to kill your joys with love', with the personification of 'heaven' also suggesting that they are being punished by God for their behaviour); he describes how their deaths will affect both families ('all are punish'd') and uses personification to suggest the sadness that their deaths have brought ('The sun, for sorrow, will not show his head'); Lady Capulet refers to 'the people in the street', suggesting that the tragedy has affected everyone; she also suggests that the sight of their deaths will kill her (the simile, 'This sight of death is as a bell / That warns my old age to a sepulchre.'), and this parallels Lord Montague's announcement that his wife has died from grief over Romeo's banishment; Lord Capulet makes amends with Lord Montague, calling him 'brother' (a sign of friendship but also a reference to Romeo and Juliet's marriage) and symbolically requesting 'give me thy hand'; Lord Montague also offers amends by stating that he will erect a statue of Juliet 'in pure gold'; Lord Capulet agrees with the wish to honour their children's love and admits the families' blame for their deaths ('As rich shall Romeo's by his lady's lie, / Poor sacrifices of our enmity!'); the final rhyming couplet of the play, spoken by the Prince, emphasises the mood of tragedy: 'For never was a story of more woe / Than this of Juliet and her Romeo'.

Comic Strip

'Then I defy you, stars!'

Pages 20–21

Revise 1

a) False b) False c) True d) True

Revise 2

Answers should include: a) the majority of 14th-century Italian society would have been Catholic; Shakespeare shows this through references to confession, the marriage ceremony, the families' 'eye for an eye' attitude of retaliation, and the trust Romeo and Juliet have in Friar Laurence; the characters' speech also includes a lot of religious imagery that emphasises ideas about love and death; b) society would have been patriarchal (controlled by men) and this can be seen in the presentation of Lord Capulet as head of his family, ideas linking to having an heir, the importance of Juliet having a husband (as well as the marriage being arranged by her father and his reaction when she refuses) and institutions like the Church and the State being led by men (Friar Laurence and Prince Escalus); c) linking to patriarchy, the male characters are often fighting for status (within and between the families) such as Lord Capulet and Lord Montague in Act 1 scene 1 or Tybalt and Lord Capulet in Act 1 scene 5; Juliet's proposed marriage to Paris is also related to gaining status.

Revise 3

Answers might include: initially, mirroring his words in Act 1 scene 2, Capulet speaks as if marriage is Juliet's choice (the adjective in 'I will make a desperate tender' implies that, although he wants her to marry Paris, it is up to her), which would have been quite unusual but shows his care and respect for his daughter; however, a more controlling attitude to his daughter's future is signalled when he acknowledges that it is his right to choose her husband ('I think she will be rul'd

In all respects by me'), despite the verb 'think' allowing the idea that Juliet may not agree; he soon becomes more dominant, showing less respect for Juliet, by announcing 'She shall be married to this noble earl' (with the modal verb 'shall' now removing Juliet's choice); Capulet suddenly wants to rush Juliet into marriage and this 'haste', contrasting with his attitude in Act 1 scene 2, is emphasised by the use of time (it is Monday night and the wedding is arranged for Thursday).

Extend

Answers might explore: Lord Capulet sees Juliet as a traditionally weak and compliant female ('Thy tempest-tossed body') so is surprised and angry when she stands up to him ('What is this?'); he cannot understand Juliet's refusal to marry Paris because he sees the man as having high status ('worthy'); he refers to his patriarchal rights to marry Juliet to whom he pleases ('I will drag thee on a hurdle thither'); his insults draw on social and religious expectations of female purity, calling her a prostitute ('baggage') for disobeying him; he is aware of Juliet's financial vulnerability if cut off from the family and uses this to force her to marry Paris ('hang! Beg! Starve! Die in the streets!'); he reacts with fury – partly highlighted by the use of blasphemy – when the other women (including the Nurse who is also of a much lower class) try to calm him down: 'Hold your tongue, / Good prudence! Smatter with your gossips', 'God's bread! it makes me mad!'.

Pages 22–23

Revise 1

a) False b) True c) True d) True

Revise 2

Answers should include: the 15th-century Wars of the Roses, centred around two rival families fighting for control of the English throne, can be seen in the conflict between the Capulets and the Montagues ('Two households, both alike in dignity, / … From ancient grudge break to new mutiny'); due to high taxes and lack of food, there was civil unrest in England and this can be reflected in the mass brawling that takes place between the families on the streets of Verona ('Prince: Rebellious subjects, enemies to peace, / Profaners of this neighbour-stained steel' [I i]).

Revise 3

Answers might include: she makes bawdy innuendos, such as the suggestion that she lost her virginity at 13 ('Now by my maidenhead at twelve year old') and her reference to getting pregnant ('Women grow by men'); she jokes about her aged appearance ('I'll lay fourteen of my teeth / And yet, to my teen be it spoken, I have but four'); she talks in a humorously protracted or rambling way which annoys others (her long speech, full of filler phrases such as 'I remember it well … I shall never forget it … But as I said … and, by my holidame …' leads Lady Capulet to say, 'Enough of this; I pray thee, hold thy peace.'); she makes several references to breasts through images of weaning ('I would say thou hadst suck'd wisdom from thy teat') which could have been emphasised through comic performance as the Nurse would have been played by a man.

Extend

Answers might explore: his use of sexual innuendos and puns (e.g. linking dealing with unrequited love to getting rid of an erection: 'Prick love for pricking, and you beat love down' [I iv]); referring to women getting used to sex ('Making them women of good carriage' [I iv]); comparing Rosaline to a fruit that looks like a vagina and linking Romeo to a fruit whose name links to sex ('O that she were / An open-arse and thou a poperin pear' [II i]); referring to fish eggs to suggest that Romeo has ejaculated inside Rosaline ('Without his roe' [II iv]); telling a jokey story that could be interpreted as being about sex ('hide his bauble in a hole' [II iv]); pretending to apologise when he makes rude remarks ('we'll draw thee from the mire / Of – save your reverence – love' [I iv]); references to vaginas ('tender thing' [I iv], 'the demesnes that there adjacent lie', 'his mistress' circle' [II i]) and erections ('letting it there stand … raise up him' [II i], 'the prick of noon' [II iv]); references to prostitution (he suggests the Nurse runs a brothel, 'A bawd!', and makes a pun linked to words for prostitutes: 'something stale and hoar' [II iv]).

Pages 24–25

Revise 1

Answers should include: a tragedy is a story that features sad or distressing events, the downfall of a central figure through a flaw in their character, and an unhappy ending. (Romeo and Juliet features several deaths and traumatic experiences, Romeo and Juliet's love and impulsiveness lead to their demise, and the play ends with their deaths although there is some redemption through the rival families' reconciliation.)

Revise 2

Answers should include: a) Shakespeare's soliloquies let the audience know what a character is truly feeling which, in Romeo and Juliet, often heightens the sense of tragedy or passion on stage (for example, Juliet's desperation and terror as she prepares to fake her own death); b) disguise is often used to create dramatic irony (the sense of secrecy means the audience is aware of some things that the characters are not), for example, when Romeo first falls in love with Juliet and is unaware that she is a Capulet; c) violence is used to establish themes of conflict and tragedy, and also to keep the audience engaged through shock and excitement (such as the fight between Paris and Romeo which contrasts with the initial mood of grief, as well as creating tragedy when Romeo realises he has killed someone who loved Juliet; this similarity with Paris also foreshadows his own tragic death).

Revise 3

Answers might include: the use of a sonnet (the traditional form of a love poem) to foretell the deaths of Romeo and Juliet; lines 5 and 6 introducing the idea that the lovers are destined to die (the metaphors 'fatal loins … star-cross'd'); the suggestion that the main characters will experience difficulties ('misadventur'd piteous overthrows … fearful passage'), leading to their suicide ('take their life'); repeated references to their deaths ('their death-mark'd love', 'their children's end'); the reference to timing ('the two hours' traffic of our stage') to introduce the way Shakespeare keeps quickly moving events forward to highlight the idea that their deaths cannot be stopped.

Extend

Answers might explore: Mercutio's mockery of Benvolio at the start of Act 3 scene 1 and the use of wordplay in 'as soon moved to be moody, and as soon moody to be moved ... thou wilt quarrel with a man for cracking nuts, having no other reason but because thou hast hazel eyes' and how this contrasts with the increasingly serious mood later in the scene as he comes into conflict with Tybalt ('Tybalt, you rat-catcher, will you walk?') and dies cursing the families' rivalry ('A plague o' both your houses') and tragically describing his own injuries (the mixture of pathos and wordplay in 'you shall find me a grave man'); the shocking deaths at the end of Act 3 scene 1 (first Mercutio then Tybalt), the pronouncement of Romeo's punishment ('Let Romeo hence in haste, / Else, when he is found, that hour is his last') and how this creates tragic dramatic irony in Act 3 scene 2 as Juliet, innocently, describes her love for Romeo ('and Romeo / Leap to these arms') and her hopes (the metaphor 'I have bought the mansion of a love / But not possess'd it'); the relaxed scene in Act 4 scene 4 where the Nurse and Lady Capulet joke with Lord Capulet (the Nurse calls him a 'cot-queen' for getting involved in the wedding preparations, and Lady Capulet refers to his amorous past: 'you have been a mouse-hunt in your time'), and he jokes with the servants ('A merry whoreson, ha! / Thou shalt be loggerhead'), and how this contrasts with the tragic melodrama when Juliet is discovered apparently dead (such as Lady Capulet's repeated exclamation 'she's dead, she's dead, she's dead!' and Lord Capulet's simile: 'Death lies on her like an untimely frost').

Pages 26–27

Revise 1

Answers should include: the adjectives 'heavy' and 'private' suggest he is unhappy and isolates himself (linking to his unrequited love for Rosaline); as well as representing his despair, the day and night imagery could suggest that he indulges in his unhappiness.

Revise 2

Answers should include: a) the metaphor shows he is miserable and that his unrequited love oppresses him to the point where he feels he cannot be rid of it; b) as well as showing that he is romantic and brave, the lines could suggest he is spontaneous and reckless; c) these lines show Romeo's playful and witty side, speaking in riddles to the Nurse rather than revealing his identity.

Revise 3

Answers might include: he is romantic ('the exchange of joy'); his reference to religion ('close our hands with holy words') suggests he has the expected morals of the time as well as showing his faithfulness towards Juliet; the use of personification in 'love-devouring death do what he dare' shows that Romeo is reckless to the dangers of what

he is doing and suggests he has an idealistic, naïve view of love.

Extend

Answers might explore: Act 1 scene 1 presents Romeo as someone who is ruled by his heart rather than his mind (the use of oxymorons, such as 'Misshapen chaos of well-seeming forms', shows how his feelings cause confusion rather than clarity in his mind); his passion for Rosaline ('O she is rich in beauty') means his sudden love for Juliet in Act 1 scene 5 ('For I ne'er saw true beauty till this night') could make him seem fickle (something raised by Friar Laurence in Act 2 scene 3); he is presented as being fated to die ('Some consequence yet hanging in the stars') yet he also ignores his instinct of danger, making him appear reckless; he doesn't listen to advice (telling Friar Laurence to 'chide not' and ignoring his warning that 'they stumble that run fast').

Comic Strip

'With love's light wings did I o'er-perch these walls, / For stony limits cannot hold love out.'

Pages 28–29

Revise 1

Answers might include: 'Ha! Banishment! Be merciful, say "death". / For exile hath more terror in his look'; 'There is no world without Verona walls / But purgatory, torture, hell itself'; 'Calling death banishment / Thou cut'st my head off with a golden axe'; 'Heaven is here, / Where Juliet lives'; 'every unworthy thing, / Live here in heaven and may look on her, / But Romeo may not.'

Revise 2

Answers should include: a) Romeo tries to be friendly (the adjective 'good' and the adverb 'dearly') and peaceful (using 'satisfied' to suggest they should not fight); b) he feels guilty for Mercutio's death and sees himself as dishonourable for not fighting (the metaphor 'soften'd valour's steel'), blaming this on the weakness ('effeminate') of love ('thy beauty'); c) he feels despair ('dark our woes') but can also be seen as brave or reckless (staying in Verona despite it getting more 'light').

Revise 3

Answers might include: relating to traditional expectations of courtly love, Romeo makes many references to Juliet's beauty; metaphor is used to suggest Juliet's beauty is powerful enough to transform places ('her beauty makes / This vault a feasting presence, full of light'); personification suggests her beauty is stronger than death ('Death ... Hath had no power yet upon thy beauty') and another metaphor is used to compare her beauty to a flag of victory ('beauty's ensign'); he calls Juliet 'Dear'; perhaps linking to traditional marriage vows, he pledges to die with her so they can be together for eternity ('here, will I remain ... O, here / Will I set up my everlasting rest').

Extend

Answers might explore: Romeo's language in Act 3 scene 3 contains many references to death, perhaps hinting at his suicidal intent later in the play ('Hadst thou no poison mix'd, no sharp-ground knife, / No sudden mean of death'); in Act 5 scene 1, Balthasar

comments on how Romeo looks like he is going to do something reckless ('Your looks are pale and wild and do import / Some misadventure'); his decision to kill himself is almost instant ('O mischief thou art swift / To enter in the thoughts of desperate men!'); his vivid description of a fast-working poison adds to this recklessness ('And that the trunk may be discharg'd of breath / As violently as hasty powder fir'd'), as does the fact that the Apothecary says it is illegal for Romeo to buy poison; in Act 5 scene 3, worried that Balthasar will stop him from committing suicide, he threatens to 'tear thee joint by joint' if he returns to the tomb; he describes himself as 'savage-wild' and compares himself to 'empty tigers or the roaring sea'; his desperation to kill himself next to Juliet leads him to fight and kill Paris ('urging me to fury ... Wilt thou provoke me?').

Comic Strip

'Calling death banishment, / Thou cut'st my head off with a golden axe / And smilest upon the stroke that murders me.'

Pages 30–31

Revise 1

Answers should include: Juliet is not interested in marriage and has never considered it; meeting Romeo changes her thoughts and her behaviour.

Revise 2

Answers should include: a) she does not have a close relationship with her mother ('Madam' is quite formal) but she is respectful and obedient ('your will'); b) although she is superior to the Nurse (giving her the order 'Go ask his name'), she has a closer relationship with her than she does with her parents and confides in her (the emotional simile); c) she quickly falls in love with Romeo, wants to marry him, and is willing to do anything for him, such as risk her family's anger or give up her current life ('no longer be a Capulet').

Revise 3

Answers might include: Juliet is cautious (the list and repetition in 'It is too rash, too unadvised, too sudden') and doesn't fully trust Romeo ('if thou meanest not well'), perhaps linking to her age or even to an awareness of men's attitudes to sex and the social expectations of women's purity at the time; she is romantic and hopes the love she and Romeo have will grow (the 'bud of love' metaphor); she is honest about her feelings and speaks passionately (the similes linked to the sea, the falconry imagery); despite her caution, she is also reckless when she suggests they get married ('Where and what time thou wilt perform the rite'), although the inclusion of religious language also shows that she is following moral expectations; despite being quite headstrong, she also adheres to gender expectations of the time, accepting Romeo as her 'lord' whom she will 'follow'; she is worried for Romeo's safety ('I would have thee gone').

Extend

Answers might explore: The contradictory nature of Juliet's character is introduced through her parents' conflicting opinions about her in Act 1 scene 2 and Act 1 scene 3 (to Lord Capulet, she seems too young and innocent for marriage but to Lady Capulet, she is ready for motherhood); she is presented as obedient (suggesting in Act 1 scene 3 that she will only fall in love in line with her parents' wishes: 'no more deep will I endart mine eye / Than your consent gives strength to make it fly') but then she falls in love with a Montague in Act 1 scene 5 ('My only love sprung from my only hate!'); in Act 2 scene 5 she relies upon the Nurse and is affectionate towards her ('O honey Nurse') but she is also critical of her ('Unwieldy, slow, heavy, and pale as lead'); she isn't sure that she can trust Romeo in Act 2 scene 2 ('Lest that thy love prove likewise variable') but her passionate recklessness is seen the following day when she meets him to be married in Act 2 scene 6 ('But my true love is grown to such excess').

Comic Strip

'O Romeo, Romeo! wherefore art thou Romeo? / Deny thy father and refuse thy name'

Pages 32–33

Revise 1

Answers should include: the use of the pronoun 'my' suggests he is her one and only love; the verb phrase 'give me' shows her eagerness in relation to him coming to consummate their marriage; the adjectives 'gentle' and 'loving' link to the happiness that Romeo makes her feel; the references to darkness and 'night' show the secrets she is willing to keep in order to be with him.

Revise 2

Answers should include: **a)** thinking Romeo is dead, she repeats the idea of being heartbroken and uses hyperbole (the prison image, suggesting she will never leave the house again or will perhaps wear a funeral veil forever) to emphasise her grief; **b)** the list shows the strength of their relationship by portraying the different things they mean to each other, while the modal verb 'must' and the metaphor 'in a minute there are many days' convey her desperation to see him again; **c)** using the double meaning created by the parenthetic dashes, she pretends to hate Romeo for killing Tybalt ('till I behold him – dead') while secretly pledging her love for him (the metaphor 'dead – / Is my poor heart').

Revise 3

Answers might include: thinking she has lost Romeo and must marry Paris, she is miserable and full of despair (the list and repetition in 'Come weep with me; past hope, past cure, past help!'); she is suicidal ('And with this knife I'll help it presently') and makes several references to killing herself if the Friar cannot help her; linking to the importance of the church at the time, she sees marrying Paris as going against religion ('God join'd my heart and Romeo's') as well as against her emotions (the metaphor 'my true heart with treacherous revolt'); she is desperate and will do anything to avoid marrying Paris (indicated by the list of frightening deeds: 'chain me with roaring bears …'); she wants to stay faithful, in body as well as in mind, to Romeo (the metaphor 'live an unstain'd wife to my sweet love').

Extend

Answers might explore: in Act 3 scene 5, she begs her father not to marry her to

Paris ('Good father, I beseech you on my knees') and pleads for her mother's help ('O, sweet my mother, cast me not away!'); she sees no one as having any 'pity' for her and talks of suicide ('make the bridal bed / In that dim monument where Tybalt lies') but is ignored; the use of repeated questions when asking the Nurse for help ('What say'st thou? Hast thou not a word of joy?') emphasises her desperation; she feels betrayed by the Nurse's lack of help ('Ancient damnation! O most wicked fiend') and can no longer rely on her ('Thou and my bosom henceforth shall be twain'); the false way in which Juliet speaks to the Nurse shows that she is now on her own and this is repeated in her pretence to Lady Capulet in Act 4 scene 3; before taking the potion, she thinks of calling to the Nurse but believes no one can help her ('What should she do here? / My dismal scene I needs must act alone.') and this is emphasised by her dialogue being a soliloquy; the long description of her fears and paranoia (that the potion won't work, that Friar Laurence is actually trying to kill her, etc.) reflect her loneliness; despite this, she takes the potion as it is the only chance she has to be with Romeo ('Romeo, Romeo, Romeo, here's drink! I drink to thee!').

Comic Strip

'O happy dagger. / This is thy sheath.'

Pages 34–35

Revise 1

Answers should include: Mercutio and Romeo are close friends, with Romeo confiding in him (the metaphor 'I sink'); Mercutio often makes rude jokes about things, using wordplay to turn Romeo's comment about unrequited love into a reference to sex ('burden love') and the vagina ('tender thing').

Revise 2

Answers should include: **a)** Mercutio creates a sexual pun with the word meddle (which was an old phrase for sexual intercourse) and refers to the medlar fruit (which was said to resemble female genitalia) to suggest that Romeo is waiting for Rosaline to have sex with him; he continues to use the fruit to joke about Rosaline and Romeo having a sexual relationship by using a slang term for the medlar ('open-arse') and combining it with a poperin (a pear which was said to look like a penis and whose name could sound like a reference to intercourse: pop her in); **b)** Mercutio uses puns to insult the Nurse, primarily using 'hoar' (meaning old) to sound like 'whore'; his joke is about an old hare not being worth buying for meat because it will be going mouldy and won't taste very nice, but it implies that the Nurse is an old prostitute ('hoar') who has gone mouldy ('it hoars') and is physically used up through sex ('spent') so isn't worth paying for ('too much').

Revise 3

Answers might include: Mercutio shows bitterness at losing his life to the grudge between the Capulets and Montagues (he is from neither family), repeatedly cursing the families: 'A plague o' both your houses';

he accepts that he has no hope of living, saying simply 'I am sped' and later describing himself as 'worms' meat'; fulfilling his comic role, he makes morbid jokes about his death, comparing his wound to 'a church door' (which his dead body will be taken through at his funeral) and saying that, by tomorrow, he will be a 'grave man' (a pun on 'serious' and a place of burial); he is critical of Tybalt, calling him a 'cat' (repeated from earlier in Act 3 scene 1) and 'a braggart, a rogue, a villain'; he blames Romeo ('Why the devil came you between us? I was hurt under your arm').

Extend

Answers might explore: Mercutio is built up as a likeable comic character, only to be suddenly killed; his first scene (Act 1 scene 4) presents him as cheerful ('we must have you dance') and having a rude sense of humour (such as his use of wordplay in 'Prick love for pricking and you beat love down') which would appeal to some of the audience; however, his language (prick/stab) also foreshadows his death which links to the play's theme of fate; his lines suggest an energetic or excitable performance (such as 'Nay, I'll conjure too: / Romeo! Humours! Madman! Passion! Lover!' [I Ii]), contrasting with Romeo's often serious, philosophical character, which makes his death more unexpected; his long, humorous speeches (such as his description of Queen Mab) contrast with the brevity of his speech when he is dying; he makes fun of characters like Benvolio, Romeo and the Nurse (for example in II iv and III i), and this contrasts with his reliance on Benvolio and his anger and disappointment with Romeo in his death scene; he seems very confident at the start of Act 3 scene 1 ('By my heel, I care not'), contrasting with his hollow humour ('grave man') when he realises he is dying.

Comic Strip

'Marry, farewell! I pray you, sir, what saucy merchant was this, that was so full of his ropery?'

Pages 36–37

Revise 1

Answers should include: Tybalt is aggressive ('look upon thy death'); he uses animal imagery to belittle Benvolio and present himself as more masculine than others ('heartless hinds' means a female deer with no fighting spirit); the use of animal imagery also shows disdain for people of a lower class (the fighting servants); his use of a rhetorical question and imperatives increases his sense of dominance.

Revise 2

Answers might include: Tybalt seems aggressive and easily angered (particularly his use of nouns in 'Uncle, this is a Montague, our foe: / A villain that is hither come in spite'), which is highlighted by Lord Capulet's contrasting calm; he is narrow-minded and unable to see beyond the families' grudge, repeating that Romeo is a 'villain', in contrast with Lord Capulet saying he has heard Romeo is 'virtuous and well-govern'd'; he seems unable to control himself ('I'll not endure him') and is disrespectful to his uncle as he contradicts him ('Why, uncle, 'tis a shame'); Lord Capulet's fury shows that

Tybalt is still only young ('What, goodman boy!') and, ultimately, must obey his family ('I'll make you quiet'); he is vengeful ('this intrusion shall / Now seeming sweet, convert to bitt'rest gall').

Revise 3

Answers might include: matching his social status, Tybalt is able to be polite and respectful, even to Montagues ('Gentlemen, good e'en'), although this may simply be an act as he is trying to find out Romeo's whereabouts; he is calm, ignoring Mercutio's taunts ('Well, peace be with you, sir: here comes my man'); however, he is aggressive towards Romeo ('thou art a villain') and vengeful ('Boy, this shall not excuse the injuries / That thou hast done me; therefore turn and draw'), with his response being very extreme given that Romeo only went to the party uninvited; Tybalt's exit after killing Mercutio can be seen as either cowardly or sensible, but his anger seems uncontrollable, leading him to return to the scene (with Benvolio describing him as 'the furious Tybalt back again').

Extend

Answers might explore: Benvolio presents him as aggressive ('The fiery Tybalt' [I i]); Lord Capulet presents him as aggressive but also arrogant and over-confident ('You will set cock-a-hoop! you'll be the man … You are a princox' [I v]); in Act 2 scene 4, Mercutio acknowledges that Tybalt is a good swordsman but also mocks him for his fighting style ('he fights as you sing prick-song') and suggests he's effeminate ('the very butcher of a silk button') and always trying to sound fashionable and of a higher status ('these new tuners of accents'); however, after his death, the Nurse describes him as kind, polite and honourable: 'the best friend I had! / O courteous Tybalt! honest gentleman!' [III ii]; Juliet was close to Tybalt, describing him as her 'dear-loved cousin' [III ii], and Lord Capulet tells Paris that Juliet 'loved her kinsman Tybalt dearly' [III iv].

Comic Strip

'Romeo, the love I bear thee can afford / No better term than this: thou art a villain.'

Pages 38–39

Revise 1

Answers should include: Lord Capulet appears bad tempered and aggressive (the imperative about his sword); Lady Capulet seems to be less violent (questioning his wish for his sword); she also mocks her husband's age ('a crutch', suggesting he is too old to be fighting), implying that she is quite a lot younger than he is.

Revise 2

Answers should include: Lord Capulet believes it is too early for Juliet to get married (the fruit metaphor) because she is young and innocent ('a stranger in the world'); he seems more cautious and caring about Juliet's wellbeing; Lady Capulet thinks Juliet should already be married (the imperative 'think of marriage now') and have children ('Younger than you … already mothers'); she puts pressure on Juliet and seems to base her opinions more on social expectations ('Here in Verona, ladies of esteem') than concern for her daughter.

Revise 3

Answers might include: in Act 3 scene 1, she demands that Romeo is executed for killing Tybalt: 'Romeo slew Tybalt. Romeo must not live'; linking to the dominant Catholic religion of the play's setting, her vengeance seems to be based on the Old Testament idea of 'an eye for an eye' ('For blood of ours, shed blood of Montague'); in Act 3 scene 5, she is angry that Romeo has only been banished (her emotive adjectives and verbs in 'the villain lives which slaughter'd him … the traitor murderer lives'); the modal verb 'will' in 'We will have vengeance for it' shows her determination to get revenge; she plans to have Romeo poisoned ('give him such an unaccustom'd dram / That he shall soon keep Tybalt company', foreshadowing his actual suicide in Act 5) and believes that such vengeance will heal Juliet's grief ('Then weep no more … then, I hope, thou wilt be satisfied').

Extend

Answers might explore: in Act 1 scene 2, Paris is having to ask Lord Capulet's permission to marry Juliet ('But now, my lord, what say you to my suit?'); in Act 1 scene 5, he welcomes guests to the party and gives orders to servants and musicians ('You are welcome, gentlemen! come, musicians, play. / A hall, a hall, give room!'); he argues with Tybalt and reminds him that the party is at 'my house', ordering Tybalt to accept Romeo's presence ('he shall be endur'd'), and insulting and threatening Tybalt for daring to question his authority ('You are a princox: go: Be quiet, or … I'll make you quiet'); after Tybalt's death, Capulet decides that Juliet should marry Paris (first planning to ask her, 'desperate tender', then deciding to tell her, 'I think she will be rul'd / In all respects by me; nay, more, I doubt it not' [III iv]); he gives his wife orders ('Go you to Juliet ere you go to bed, / Prepare her, wife' [III iv]); as in his argument with Tybalt, when his traditional authority as the head of the house is questioned, Lord Capulet loses his temper ('God's bread, it makes me mad!' [III v]); he uses his power over Juliet to try to force her to get married ('Beg! Starve! Die in the streets! / For by my soul I'll ne'er acknowledge thee' [III v]); in Act 4 scenes 2 and 4, he is shown giving orders to Juliet, his wife, the Nurse and the servants; as the head of the house, the idea of an heir is important, and this influences his grief in Act 4 scene 5 ('Death is my heir'); ultimately, it is Lord Capulet who seeks to end the grudge between the two families ('O brother Montague, give me thy hand [V iii]).

Comic Strip

'I would the fool were married to her grave!'

Pages 40–41

Revise 1

Answers should include: Paris is grieving over Juliet's death and uses a flower metaphor to describe her beauty and innocence (as well as repeating the adjective 'sweet' to show his love for her); he suggests his love lasts beyond her death as he will visit her tomb 'nightly' to water the flowers he has laid, using his 'tears distill'd by moans' if necessary.

Revise 2

Answers might include: a) the metaphor 'he's a man of wax' suggests that the Nurse thinks Paris is perfect, like a wax model, while the metaphor 'he's a flower' suggests she thinks he is handsome but also gentle; b) her pet names for Juliet such as 'lamb' and 'ladybird' suggest their closeness and her desire to care for her; stories of Juliet's childhood in lines like 'She could have run and waddled all about' show how fond she is of her; her wish for Juliet to find love ('Go, girl, seek happy nights to happy days') indicates that she wants her to be happy; c) she is given orders by Lady Capulet ('give leave awhile … come back again'); her lack of upper-class respectability is shown by her jokes about her age ('I have but four [teeth]') and the fact that she refers to the loss of her virginity in front of her respectable employer ('by my maidenhead at twelve year old'); she also jokes about Juliet getting pregnant ('Women grow by men'); she uses lots of filler phrases that make her sound comic and rambling such as 'But as I said', 'I remember it well' and 'I never shall forget it', and she sounds crude because she often refers to parts of the body such as 'the nipple / Of my dug' and the simile 'as big as a young cockerel's stone [testicle]'.

Revise 3

Answers might include: humour is created through her complaint about Mercutio linking her to prostitution ('Scurvy knave! I am none of his flirt-gills'); this is developed through the character of her servant Peter who uses double meanings to turn the Nurse's words about being mocked by Mercutio ('at his pleasure') into a suggestion that she has had sex with Mercutio; Peter adds a crude innuendo ('my weapon should quickly have been out') to joke that he'd also have sex with her; anger at Peter's crudeness could also create humour ('I am so vexed that every part of me quivers'), especially as any references to the Nurse's body could link to the Elizabethan audience's awareness that she is being played, to comic effect, by a man; at the end of the scene, she starts to inappropriately gossip with Romeo, beginning a story about Juliet's childhood, using a 'toad' simile to refer to Juliet's feelings about Paris, nearly swearing ('R is for the – ' stopping herself from saying 'arse'), and confusing her words (saying 'sententious', which means moral and pompous, instead of 'sentence'); she shows a more serious side in her protection of Juliet, reminding Romeo that Juliet is 'young'; she also refers to the social expectations of a gentleman, by telling him that to mislead Juliet (the metaphor 'lead her into a fool's paradise' and the phrase 'deal double') would be 'a very gross kind of behaviour, … an ill thing … and very weak dealing'.

Extend

Answers might explore: in Act 1 scene 3, the Nurse's love for Juliet contrasts with the crude and humorous speech that was typical of Shakespeare's comic characters (see answers to the Revise 2 task above); in Act 2 scene 5, she comically annoys Juliet by deliberately making her wait for news of Romeo ('I am a-weary, give me leave awhile. / Fie, how my bones ache. What a jaunt have I had!', and her rambling description of Romeo's qualities), as well as later making a sexual joke about Juliet losing her virginity to Romeo ('you shall bear the burden soon at night'); however, she also plays the role of Juliet's confidant, organising the marriage and the wedding night ('Hie you to church'); she begins Act 4 scene 5 making jokes about Juliet being sleepy ('You slug-a-bed!') and how she'll spend her wedding night making love to Paris ('you shall rest but little!') but this turns to grief when she believes Juliet is dead ('Never was seen so black a day as this' and repeating 'lamentable day' and 'woeful day').

Comic Strip

'Beshrew my very heart, / I think you are happy in this second match.'

Pages 42–43

Revise 1

Answers should include: Benvolio is close to Romeo and feels sorry for him ('weep'); he empathises with Romeo's feelings of unrequited love (the metaphor 'thy good heart's oppression'); Romeo's questions suggest he doesn't realise how understanding Benvolio is; their sharing of the iambic pentameter emphasises their closeness.

Revise 2

Answers might include: a) Benvolio's opening speech ('let's retire … we shall not scape a brawl … the mad blood stirring') suggests he wants to avoid any conflict with the Capulets, but Mercutio talks as if Benvolio is always stirred to violence: 'draws him on the drawer, when indeed there is no need … thou art as hot a Jack in thy mood as any in Italy' and continually repeats the word 'quarrel' in relation to Benvolio; b) he speaks respectfully ('O noble Prince') and supports Romeo ('with gentle breath, calm look, knees humbly bow'd'), but he appears to hide the fact that Mercutio began the fight with Tybalt ('deaf to peace, but that he tilts / With piercing steel at bold Mercutio's breast') and Lady Capulet accuses him of lying: 'Affection makes him false. He speaks not true'.

Revise 3

Answers might include: the Friar defends his actions by saying that Juliet would have committed suicide ('Or in my cell there would she kill herself') which was deemed a sin at the time; he recounts how he tried to resolve the situation ('Came I … meaning to keep her closely at my cell'); he uses the verb 'entreated' to suggest he tried his best to help Juliet; he also refers to the play's events ('Tybalt's doomsday, whose untimely death / Banish'd the new-made bridegroom … would have married her perforce / To County Paris') to suggest that fate was against them; he admits that he 'married them' and that he planned the fake death ('A sleeping potion, which so took effect / As I intended'); he says he is willing to be punished by death: 'let my old life / Be sacrific'd, some hour before his time / Unto the rigour of severest law' (although the verb 'sacrific'd' and the phrase 'before his time' suggest he does not deserve the punishment).

Extend

Ideas might explore: in Act 2 scene 3, Friar Laurence worries about the inconstancy of Romeo's heart ('Is Rosaline, whom thou didst love so dear, / So soon forsaken?') yet he agrees to marry them ('I'll thy assistant be'); his

hope that 'this alliance may so happy prove, / To turn your households' rancour to pure love' seems naïve in the context of all the conflict that Shakespeare has already presented on stage; he warns Romeo about not rushing into things ('Wisely and slow; they stumble that run fast' [II iii]) and is aware that the marriage could bring disaster ('These violent delights have violent ends' [II vi]) but marries the lovers the same day; in Act 4 scene 1, he disapproves of the speed and arrangement of Juliet's marriage to Paris ('Uneven is the course. I like it not.') but agrees to it, even though it would be bigamy and therefore illegal and sinful; rather than tell the truth (even though, in his role, he encourages people to take confession), he comes up with the sleeping potion plan, calling it 'A thing like death to chide away this shame', suggesting he is thinking about his own reputation as much as Juliet's happiness; even in Act 5 scene 3, rather than have the truth revealed, he tries to convince Juliet to enter a nunnery ('I'll dispose of thee / Among a sisterhood of holy nuns'); worried about the consequences to his own life ('I dare no longer stay'), he leaves Juliet to her fate despite her being in his religious care (which he acknowledges when he calls her 'daughter' [IV i]).

Comic Strip

'These violent delights have violent ends.'

Pages 44–45

Revise 1

Answers should include: Romeo's unrequited love for Rosaline; Romeo and Juliet's forbidden love, affected by their families' grudge, Romeo's banishment and Juliet's arranged marriage to Paris; Paris's unrequited love for Juliet and the initial obstacle of Lord Capulet believing his daughter is too young to get married.

Revise 2

Answers might include: a) the metaphor 'Juliet is the sun'; the celestial imagery in 'The brightness of her cheek would shame those stars, / As daylight doth a lamp' and 'bright angel'; the precious and sensual imagery in 'How silver-sweet sound lovers' tongues by night', and the natural imagery in 'by yonder blessed moon I swear, / That tips with silver all these fruit-tree tops' and 'this bud of love, by summer's ripening breath, / May prove a beauteous flower' all suggest that love transforms people and things for the better; b) the metaphor 'With love's light wings did I o'er-perch these walls; / For stony limits cannot hold love out' suggests nothing can stop love; c) the use of future tense in 'be but sworn my love / And I'll no longer be a Capulet' and 'Call me but love, and I'll be new baptis'd', and the brave verbs in 'what love can do, that dares love attempt' show the lovers' willingness to do anything for each other, while the list, repetition and simile in 'It is too rash, too unadvis'd, too sudden, / Too like the lightning' show Juliet's fear that she has been too impulsive.

Revise 3

Answers might include: the religious imagery matches the Catholic faith that was dominant in Italy at the time, making their love seem morally right or even blessed by God;

Romeo's verb 'profane' is used to suggest that Juliet seems holy and deserves more love than he can give; this is continued with the metaphors 'holy shrine' and 'blushing pilgrims', suggesting his love is like worship; she responds with similar religious imagery, reinforcing the idea that their love is blessed by linking their physical contact to the 'devotion' of pilgrims (also known as palmers); they each refer to their kiss as a 'prayer' and he pledges his 'faith' to her, suggesting the depth of their love; they talk of their passion being a 'sin' but suggest it is forgiven ('purg'd') because their love is so strong.

Extend

Answers might explore: the descriptions in Act 1 scene 1 of Romeo's unhappiness due to unrequited love ('With tears augmenting the fresh morning's dew'), as well as the inner turmoil that is shown through his use of oxymorons ('O loving hate') and, in Act 1 scene 4, classical imagery ('I am too sore enpierced with his [Cupid's] shaft'); Romeo and Juliet struggling to say goodbye to each other in Act 2 scene 2 ('Parting is such sweet sorrow'); Juliet's turmoil in Act 3 scene 2 when she finds that Romeo has killed Tybalt ('Shall I speak ill of him that is my husband?'); in Act 3 scenes 2 and 3, Romeo's response to his banishment ('Heaven is here / Where Juliet lives'); Romeo referring to 'all these woes' in Act 3 scene 5, and Juliet's distress in front of her parents ('I cannot choose but ever weep'); the suicides of Romeo and Juliet in Act 5 scene 3 ('Here's to my love!', 'O happy dagger').

Comic Strip

'Parting is such sweet sorrow / That I shall say good night till it be morrow.'

Pages 46–47

Revise 1

Answers should include: the overall grudge between the Capulets and Montagues ends with the deaths of Romeo and Juliet; the conflict between Tybalt and Mercutio results in their deaths; Romeo's aggressive retaliation leads to his banishment, Juliet's arranged marriage to Paris and, ultimately, his and Juliet's suicides; Paris's aggression in Act 5 leads to his death.

Revise 2

Answers should include: a) the use of stichomythia (short alternate lines, repeating key words) makes the servants' conflict comic, as does the false respect ('sir') that they pay each other as if they were gentlemen rather than lower class; b) in contrast to his usual comic language, Mercutio's curse ('a plague') and metaphor ('worms' meat') emphasise the tragedy of his death, with the pronouns (your/ they) also highlighting how he has died for a cause that isn't even his own; c) Lord Capulet insults his daughter (linking her to prostitution, 'baggage') and shows his contempt for her ('wretch') after her refusal to marry Paris.

Revise 3

Answers might include: Mercutio, who is a higher-class relative of Prince Escalus, thinks Tybalt is insulting him by linking him to lower-class musicians ('Zounds, consort!') so brandishes his sword to suggest he would be the better fighter ('Here's my fiddlestick, here's that shall / make you dance'); Mercutio tries to provoke Tybalt by questioning his honour and implying he is a coward ('your livery' is a pun on being 'lily-livered'); Tybalt insults Romeo by suggesting that, instead of being a young gentleman, he is of low status ('thou art a villain'); Tybalt's wish to fight Romeo is based on the feeling that Romeo disrespected the Capulets by attending their party ('the injuries / That thou has done me'), linking also to how Lord Capulet humiliated him at the time; Mercutio is angered by Romeo's refusal to fight, calling it 'dishonourable, vile submission' (he is perhaps also feeling foolish, having told Tybalt that Romeo would eagerly fight him: 'he'll be your follower'); when Romeo accidentally causes Mercutio's death ('hath got his mortal hurt / In my behalf') and reflects on Tybalt's insults (the metaphor 'my reputation stain'd / With Tybalt's slander'), he feels it is honourable to either kill Tybalt or die as well ('Either thou, or I, or both must go with him'); Lady Capulet says Escalus must honour his previous ruling (in Act 1 scene 1) and have Romeo executed ('Prince, as thou art true, / For blood of ours, shed blood of Montague').

Extend

Answers might explore: the initial fight between the Capulets and Montagues in Act 1 scene 1 is linked to which family is 'better', and Lord Capulet joins in because he feels that Lord Montague is challenging his honour ('flourishes his blade in spite of me', especially the verb 'flourishes'); Tybalt thinks that Romeo has disrespected the Capulets by attending the party in Act 1 scene 5 (the verbs in 'To fleer and scorn at our solemnity?' and the nouns in 'Now, by the stock and honour of my kin'); however, Lord Capulet thinks he is being dishonoured when Tybalt argues with him (the rhetorical question 'Am I the master here, or you?') and dishonours Tybalt by mocking his youth and immaturity ('What, goodman boy!'); Lord Capulet again loses his temper in Act 3 scene 5 when he feels Juliet is disrespecting him by refusing to marry Paris ('Out, you green-sickness carrion!'), particularly as he feels he has tried to increase her own honour by finding her a husband of status (the adjectives in 'So worthy a gentleman' and 'a gentleman of noble parentage'); in Act 5 scene 3 Paris fights Romeo to uphold Tybalt's and Juliet's honour as he believes Romeo has come to 'do some villainous shame / To the dead bodies'.

Comic Strip

'Put not another sin upon my head / By urging me to fury.'

Pages 48–49

Revise 1

'Still-waking sleep, that is not what it is' (I i)	Oxymoron
'Bid a sick man in sadness make his will?' (I i)	Rhetorical question
'Shut up in prison, kept without my food' (I ii)	Metaphor
'Then "banished" / Is death mis-term'd' (III iii)	Hyperbole
'O mischief thou art swift / To enter in the thoughts of desperate men!' (V i)	Personification

Revise 2

Answers should include: a) the question shows that his turmoil comes from not knowing what his punishment will be (dramatic irony increases the audience's sympathy as they know he has been banished), while the noun 'sorrow' shows he expects it to be harsh; b) the tricolon (or pattern of three) emphasises the idea that he thinks death would be better than banishment because he cannot live without Juliet (the reference to poison and a knife also foreshadows their eventual deaths), and this is reinforced by the pun on 'mean' to suggest these ways to achieve death aren't as cruel as banishment; c) Romeo believes it is impossible ('canst not') for others to understand the degree of his emotional turmoil.

Revise 3

Answers might include: Juliet's turmoil is both emotional (personification showing that she will not stop loving Romeo: 'my true heart with treacherous revolt') and religious ('God join'd my heart' reminds the audience that she would be committing the sin and crime of bigamy); her tricolon ('past hope, past cure, past help') emphasises her feelings of desperation; she considers killing herself ('with this knife I'll help it presently … I long to die / If what thou speak'st speak not of remedy'); her list of verb phrases ('O, bid me leap …') conveys how horrified she is by the idea of marrying Paris; her awareness that she would be expected to have sexual intercourse with Paris adds to her turmoil (the metaphor 'To live an unstain'd wife to my sweet love').

Extend

Answers might explore: metaphor is used to show her terror of what she is about to do ('a faint cold fear thrills through my veins'); her awareness that she is alone ('I needs must act alone', emphasised by the modal verb); the many rhetorical questions, emphasising her turmoil and the lack of anyone to turn to; her fear and paranoia that the potion won't work, that the Friar might be trying to poison her to save his own reputation, that she will awake early and suffocate in the tomb or be driven mad and kill herself; her speech is full of disturbing imagery linked to death, such as the personification of the tomb ('whose foul mouth no healthsome air breathes in'), the use of the senses to describe horrible smells ('loathsome') and sounds (the simile 'like mandrakes torn out of the earth'), and the nightmarish image of her interfering with the dead bodies ('madly play with my forefathers' joints, / And pluck the mangled Tybalt from his shroud'); she even appears to have a vision of Tybalt ('methinks I see my cousin's ghost') wanting to kill Romeo, which leads to her speaking aloud to them ('Stay, Tybalt, stay! / Romeo, Romeo, Romeo, here's drink! I drink to thee!').

Comic Strip

'Was ever book containing such vile matter / So fairly bound? O, that deceit should dwell / In such a gorgeous palace!'

Pages 50–51

Revise 1

Answers should include: *traditional* means practices that are long established or customary, or habitually done (for example, Paris asks Capulet's permission to marry Juliet before even meeting her: 'But now my lord, what say you to my suit?'); *patriarchal* relates to a society or system that is run by men (for example, Lady Capulet follows her husband's orders: 'Go you to Juliet ere you go to bed, / Prepare her, wife').

Revise 2

Answers should include: a) the fathers are aggressive rather than peaceful (Capulet demands his sword and Montague insults him), and easily provoked rather than reasonable ('in spite of me'); this could link to Romeo's furious fight with Tybalt (as well as the aggressive behaviour of Tybalt); b) Lady Capulet tries to rush Juliet into marriage ('think of marriage now'), based on social expectations rather than common sense, and is overly romantic in her idealised presentation of love (the book metaphor); this could link to how quickly Juliet falls in love with Romeo, how she rushes into marriage and her wish to not live without him.

Revise 3

Ideas might include: the Montagues worry about Romeo's unhappiness and want to help him ('Could we but learn from whence his sorrows grow, / We would as willingly give cure as know' [I i], particularly the nouns); Lord Montague's defence of Romeo after the death of Tybalt ('Not Romeo, Prince, he was Mercutio's friend' [III i]); the news, in Act 5 scene 3, that Lady Montague has died from grief after Romeo's banishment ('Grief of my son's exile hath stopp'd her breath'); Lord Capulet's description of Juliet in Act 1 scene 2 as 'the hopeful lady of my earth' (linking to the traditional need for wealthy families to produce an heir) and his care for her wellbeing ('My child is yet a stranger in the world') and her future ('too soon marr'd are those so early made'), as well as his willingness to break with traditional custom and give her choice in her marriage ('My will to her consent is but a part'); Lady Capulet's belief in Act 1 scene 3 that marriage will be good for Juliet and her wish for her to have a happy life (the metaphor 'Verona's summer hath not such a flower'); Lord and Lady Capulet's belief that they are doing the right thing marrying Juliet to Paris and that it will make her happy ('thou hast a careful father … Hath sorted out a sudden day of joy' and the use of the list in 'Day, night, hour, tide, time, work, play, / Alone, in company, still my care hath been / To have her match'd' [III v]); the parents' grief in Act 4 scene 5 when they believe she is dead (such as the simile, 'Death lies on her like an untimely frost / Upon the sweetest flower of all the field'); Lord Capulet's horror at Juliet's suicide in Act 5 scene 3 ('O heavens! O wife, look how our daughter bleeds.') and Lady Capulet's grief making her feel close to dying ('O me! This sight of death is as a bell / That warns my old age to a sepulchre').

Extend

Answers might explore: the Montagues cannot get Romeo to confide in them ('to himself so secret and so close' [I i]) and have to ask for Benvolio's help; linking to the religious context, Romeo confides more in

Friar Laurence ('Good morrow, father … Then plainly know my heart's dear love is set / On the fair daughter of rich Capulet' [II iii]) than in his father; the Capulets' traditional use of a nurse to breastfeed and raise their daughter ('When it did taste the wormwood on the nipple / Of my dug' [I iii]) perhaps leads to Juliet confiding more in the Nurse than her parents; Act 3 scene 5 shows that Juliet's parents are capable of great anger and cruelty to their daughter ('a wretched puling fool, / A whining mammet').

Comic Strip

'Wife, we scarce thought us blest / That God had lent us but this only child; / But now I see this one is one too much, / And that we have a curse in having her.'

Pages 52–53

Revise 1

Answers should include: *fate* (or destiny) is often an element of tragedy and is the idea that our lives are predetermined by some higher power; by outlining the plot of the play, the prologue implies that everyone's lives are already written for them; the prologue suggests that, from birth, Romeo and Juliet were fated to fall in love and die ('From forth the fatal loins of these two foes / A pair of star-cross'd lovers take their life'); this idea that their fate cannot be avoided is emphasised by the description of their 'death-mark'd love'.

Revise 2

Answers should include: **a)** the use of personification suggests that Romeo feels his life is being played with by some higher power (he has been given happiness or fortune, only to have it taken away when he kills Tybalt); **b)** personification is used to show Juliet exploring the same idea, aware that she has been lucky to fall in love with Romeo but that her luck has quickly changed (it is 'fickle'); **c)** Romeo blames fate (the 'stars', linking to the Elizabethan interest in astrology and the idea that the planets influence our lives) for Juliet's (fake) death but his words suggest he thinks he can stand up to fate (emphasising the play's tragedy as the audience knows, from the prologue, that he cannot).

Revise 3

Answers might include: Romeo's several references to death (such as 'I must be gone and live, or stay and die') remind the audience that he is fated to die; an ominous (threatening) atmosphere is created by Juliet's reference to a 'meteor', which was seen as a bad omen in the 16th century and reminds the audience that a terrible fate awaits the lovers; this ominous atmosphere is increased when Romeo points out that their lives are getting worse ('more dark and dark our woes!'); dramatic irony is used in 'sweet discourses in our time to come' to emphasise what the prologue has told the audience about the fate of Romeo and Juliet; as Romeo leaves, Juliet has a vision of him 'dead in the bottom of a tomb', directly foreshadowing how she will find him in Act 5 scene 3.

Extend

Answers might explore: in Act 1 scene 4, Romeo's sense of foreboding (relating to the Elizabethan interest in astrology) as he and his friends make their way to the Capulet party ('Some consequence yet hanging in the stars / Shall bitterly begin his fearful date / With this night's revels … By some vile forfeit of untimely death') links back to what the audience is told in the prologue but also relates to how his meeting with Juliet and the anger he causes Tybalt will combine to bring about their end; Mercutio, joking about Romeo's love for Rosaline in Act 2 scene 4, describes his friend as 'already dead, stabbed with a white wench's black eye', reminding the audience that Romeo is fated or marked for death and foreshadowing how he will be killed by love (and linking to how Juliet will then stab herself); Juliet's reference to the classical gods in Act 3 scene 2 reinforces ideas of fate, with the story of Phaeton (whose recklessness led him to be killed by the god Zeus) linking to Romeo's banishment and its fatal consequences; at the start of Act 5 scene 1, Romeo dreams about Juliet finding him dead, foreshadowing the end of the play (and increasing the sense of tragedy because, in his dream, she 'breath'd such life with kisses in my lips / That I reviv'd', which he sees as a good omen).

Comic Strip

'One writ with me in sour misfortune's book!'

Pages 54–55

Revise 1

Answers might include: **Characters rushed:** Paris urges Lord Capulet to let him marry Juliet ('Younger than she are happy mothers made' [I ii]); Juliet is rushed to love and marry Paris by Lady Capulet ('think of marriage now' [I iii]); Benvolio hurries Romeo to the Capulet party ('Supper is done and we shall come too late' [I iv]); Juliet rushes the Nurse for Romeo's message ('Nay come, I pray thee, speak: good, good Nurse, speak' [II v]); on her wedding night, Juliet wishes that time would speed up ('Gallop apace you fiery-footed steeds' [III ii]); Lord Capulet rushes Juliet's wedding ('I'll have this knot knit up tomorrow morning' [IV ii]); **Decisions/events mistimed:** Romeo holds back Mercutio's arm, just as Tybalt lunges with his sword ('*Tybalt under Romeo's arm stabs Mercutio*' [III i]); Lord and Lady Capulet mistakenly think that the marriage to Paris is well-timed ('a sudden day of joy' [III v]); Friar Laurence's message misses Romeo so he thinks Juliet is dead ('Romeo / Hath had no notice of these accidents' [V ii]); Juliet fears waking too early but actually wakes too late ('Ah, what an unkind hour / Is guilty of this lamentable chance? / The lady stirs' [V iii]).

Revise 2

Answers should include: **a)** Benvolio uses the adjective 'untimely' to suggest that Mercutio should have lived longer ('That gallant spirit … Which too untimely here did scorn the earth' [III i]); **b)** the same adjective is used by Lord Capulet to describe Juliet's death (the simile, 'Death lies on her like an untimely frost' [IV v]), and he later personifies time as a surprise killer (the rhetorical question, 'Uncomfortable time, why cam'st thou now / To murder, murder our solemnity?' [IV v]); **c)** 'untimely' is repeated again when Friar Laurence describes the deaths of Romeo and Paris in Act 5 scene 3 ('here untimely lay / The noble Paris and the true Romeo dead').

Revise 3

Answers might include: in Act 3 scene 4, Paris appears eager to know if Juliet will accept his hand in marriage (Lady Capulet responds with 'I will, and know her mind early tomorrow', with the adverb adding a sense of urgency); Lord Capulet's announcement of the wedding in three days' time is unexpected and his language shows he is aware of the suddenness ('Will you be ready? Do you like this haste?'); Paris's eagerness adds to the mood of urgency ('My lord, I would that Thursday were tomorrow'); the brevity of the scene, compared to those before and after, increases the sense of suddenness and urgency; Act 4 scene 1 begins with Friar Laurence and Paris discussing the short notice of the wedding (contrasting language emphasises Paris's eagerness, 'I am nothing slow to slack his haste', with a similar contrast appearing later when Paris's reference to 'haste' is followed by the Friar's use of 'slow'); the date of the wedding ('Thursday') is repeated several times during the scene to add to the mood of urgency, and this is emphasised by the Friar saying he cannot 'prorogue' (postpone) it; Juliet's impulsive plan to kill herself ('this bloody knife') increases the idea that she is running out of time and the Friar repeats the imperative 'Hold' in his attempt to slow down the situation.

Extend

Answers might explore: Act 5, scene 1 and – especially – scene 2 are brief, moving the play quickly towards its climax, as if Romeo and Juliet's fate cannot be stopped; scene 2 also focuses on the 'Unhappy fortune' of the letter not reaching Romeo while, in scene 3, Juliet failing to wake earlier leads to Romeo's death; dramatic irony is in use throughout the act as the audience is aware that Juliet is not really dead and that mistimings are leading to tragedy; in Act 5, scene 2, the Friar's references to time ('go hence', 'Now', 'Within this three hours' and 'till') suggest that he is working against time to stop the tragedy, although he arrives at the tomb too late; the Friar's account of the events leading to Romeo's and Juliet's deaths is also full of references to time ('untimely death', 'then', 'meantime', 'the time the potion's force should cease', 'yesternight', 'prefixed hour' and 'some minute ere the time of her awakening'), emphasising how mistimings have brought about the tragedy; the Friar refers to how events 'miscarried', implying the effects of time on the lovers' deaths.

Comic Strip

'Ah what an unkind hour / Is guilty of this lamentable chance?'

Pages 56–69

Exam Questions

Use the mark scheme on page 80 to self-assess your strengths and weaknesses. Work up from the bottom, putting a tick by things you have fully accomplished, a ½ by skills that are in place but need securing, and underlining

Grade	AO1 (12 marks)	AO2 (12 marks)	AO3 (6 marks)	AO4 (4 marks)
6–7+ (19–34 marks)	A convincing, well-structured essay that answers the question fully. Quotations and references are well chosen and integrated into sentences. The response covers the whole play.	Analysis of the full range of Shakespeare's methods. Thorough exploration of the effects of these methods. Accurate range of subject terminology.	Exploration is linked to specific aspects of the play's context to show a detailed understanding.	Consistently high level of accuracy. Vocabulary and sentences are used to make ideas clear and precise.
4–5 (13–18 marks)	A clear essay that always focuses on the exam question. Quotations and references support ideas effectively. The response refers to different points in the play.	Explanation of Shakespeare's different methods. Clear understanding of the effects of these methods. Accurate use of subject terminology.	References to relevant aspects of context show a clear understanding.	Good level of accuracy. Vocabulary and sentences help to keep ideas clear.
2–3 (6–12 marks)	The essay has some good ideas that are mostly relevant. Some quotations and references are used to support the ideas.	Identification of some different methods used by Shakespeare to convey meaning. Some subject terminology.	Some awareness of how ideas in the play link to its context.	Reasonable level of accuracy. Errors do not get in the way of the essay making sense.

areas that need particular development. The estimated grade boundaries are included so you can assess your progress towards your target grade.

Pages 56–57

Answers might explore: in the extract, and when he is first introduced in Act 1 scene 1, Tybalt shows aggression based on simple hatred of the Montague family, relating to 16th-century stereotypical views that Italians were passionate and violent; in the extract, his aggression is both physical and vocal, and this can also be seen in Act 3 scene 1 where he duels and insults people's social status; linking to the social context of the two wealthy, patriarchal families, the extract shows that Tybalt's aggression arises from feelings that he has been dishonoured and this is emphasised later in Act 1 scene 5 and returned to when he confronts Romeo in Act 3 scene 1.

Pages 58–59

Answers might explore: in the extract, Juliet performs expected traditional actions of obedience towards her father (speaking to him formally and kneeling before him), similar to how she behaved towards her mother in Act 1 scene 3 before she met Romeo; the use of dramatic irony exposess the lack of closeness between Juliet and her father as the audience is aware that her remorse is not genuine and that she has no plans to follow his instructions; throughout the play, she does not have many scenes with her father and is closer to the Nurse (linking to the way young girls were brought up by a wet nurse in wealthy families); Capulet's harsh criticism of his daughter at the start of the extract links to his criticisms in Act 3 scene 5, with the focus on prostitution imagery showing that he sees his daughter's obedience as a matter of morality; he shows some care for her at the end of the extract (reminiscent of Act 1 scene 2) because she is following his orders and later displays deep grief over her death in Act 4 scene 5.

Pages 60–61

Answers might explore: in the extract, the Nurse is presented as a comic character through her rambling speech and her deliberate attempts to annoy Juliet, and this is similar to how she speaks in Act 1 scene 3; typical of comic characters in Elizabethan theatre, some of her comedy is rude/bawdy, linking to how Mercutio and Peter speak to her in Act 2 scene 4; the extract shows that she has idealised views of romance, which is also seen in the way she describes Paris in Act 1 scene 3; in the extract, her references to her role in the Capulet family, as well as the type of words she uses, show the audience that she is lower class, which was established earlier through her behaviour and speech in Act 1 scene 3; she is clearly used as a go-between, both in the extract and throughout the play, such as Act 1 scene 5, Act 2 scene 4 and Act 3 scene 3; it is clear from the extract that she loves Juliet and will do anything for her, even if it would be against the Capulets' wishes, and this is reflected in her defence of Juliet in Act 3 scene 5 and her grief in Act 4 scene 5.

Pages 62–63

Answers might explore: in the extract, linking with the Catholic context of the setting, love is presented through religious imagery as a form of worship and this can also be seen in Romeo's speech at the start of Act 2 scene 2; the extract's ideas of worship and devotion also imply that love is unique and eternal, and this can be seen in many of Romeo and Juliet's interactions but has its tragic consequences in Act 5 scene 3; the extract presents love as passionate and physical, an idea repeated in Act 3 scene 2 as Juliet awaits her wedding night but also shown in the Nurse's different sexual comments (for example, at the end of Act 2 scene 5); through the use of the sonnet form (with images of gentleness and the shared rhymes), the extract suggests love is beautiful and perfect and this is also shown in Lady Capulet's use of the sonnet form to describe Paris in Act 1 scene 3, although love also seems dangerous and impulsive such as in Act 2 scene 2; the end of the extract (the Nurse's interruption) suggests that love faces obstacles, linked to social and family expectations of the context, and this is highlighted in Act 3 scene 5.

Pages 64–65

Answers might explore: in the extract, death is presented as tragic through the change in Mercutio's usually comic character (contrasting with, for example, Act 2 scene 4) and him dying for a grudge he's not even part of; this is most clearly explored again in Act 5 scene 3; Romeo's speech in the extract presents death and killing as being linked to honour, and this is also shown by Tybalt in Act 1 scene 5; in the extract, Romeo's speech links death to fate, which is used to foreshadow further consequences, and these ideas can also be seen during Romeo and Juliet's parting in Act 3 scene 5; relating further to fate, Benvolio's words in the extract present death as 'untimely' and this is also explored in Juliet's (fake) death in Act 4 scene 5; relating to the play's religious context, death is linked to the afterlife as well as to ideas of retaliation, and the latter can be seen in Lady Capulet's speech in Act 3 scene 5.

Pages 66–67

Answers might explore: in the extract, marriage is idealised and presented as something wonderful, which is reflected in Romeo and Juliet's happiness in Act 2 scene 6 but contrasts with Lord Capulet's views in Act 1 scene 2; relating to tradition and class in the context of the play, the extract shows that marriages were arranged (often for the benefit of social status) and this is further explored in Act 3 scene 5; the extract also suggests that marriage and childbirth are social expectations for a good, moral girl (the Nurse speaks as if it's the culmination of a woman's life), and this can be seen in Lord Capulet's words in Act 4 scene 2; linking to her youth, the extract shows that Juliet is not interested in marriage, although she rushes into it in Act 2 scene 2.

Pages 68–69

Answers might explore: in the extract, inner turmoil is linked to love and this is also shown in Romeo's speeches in Act 1 scene 1 (especially his use of oxymoron); the extract shows inner turmoil creating exaggerated fears of death and madness, while it brings suicidal thoughts (seen as a sin in the play's setting) in Act 4 scene 1; the use of questioning and nightmarish imagery in the extract shows the confusion and despair caused by inner turmoil, and this is reflected in Romeo's questions and hyperbole in Act 2 scene 3; because of the context of the extract, and the situation being described, inner turmoil is also linked to loneliness and having no one to turn to, which can be seen in Juliet's death in Act 5 scene 3.